Phyllis,

to an old friend

Don

Read other books from
TWO HERONS:

Martha and the Mutt by Tad Liechty
Martha and New Horizons by Tad Liechty
Dominic's Ducks by Joanne McDonough
Dominic's Ducks at the Zoo by Joanne McDonough
Just Say So by Tad Liechty
If You Say So by Tad Liechty
The King's Cookies by Tad Liechty

Oregon State University
Corvallis, Oregon
Miami University
Oxford, Ohio

Chiang Mai University
Chiang Mai, Thailand

Don Kaufman
Mike Burgett

Printed in the United States of America.
ISBN 978-1-7322622-1-8

Published by
Berg Kaufman Publishing,
a subsidiary of Two Herons, LLC
3840 Indian Creek Road, Oxford, Ohio 45056
www.bergkaufmanpublishing.com
www.twoheronsconsulting.com
513.523.3356

Cover photos © Meg Vogel www.megvogel.com.
Book design by Carolyn Farmer.
Text typefaces: Crimson Pro, copyright © 2019, Jacques Le Bailly;
Roboto, copyright © 2016, Christian Robertson.
Display typefaces: Roboto, copyright © 2016, Christian Robertson;
Reggae One, copyright © 2021, Fontworks Inc.;
RocknRoll One, copyright © 2021, Fontworks Inc.
Crimson Pro, Reggae One, and RocknRoll One are licensed
under the SIL Open Font License, Version 1.1.
Licenses are available with an FAQ at: http://scripts.sil.org/OFL.
Roboto is licensed under the Apache License, Version 2.0.
License is available with an FAQ at: apache.org/licenses/LICENSE-2.0
All fonts downloaded from Google Fonts.

To Clark Sorensen (1944-2019),
my very great friend and fellow ponderer.
—DK

Acknowledgments

We want to thank and recognize those individuals who provided us with helpful, thoughtful reviews of early drafts of *The Monkey Brothers Adventures in Thailand*: Aaron Ames, Madeline Ames, John Berg, Steve Heffron, Patricia Kaufman, Kathy Raftery, Vickie Sorensen, and Jane Zachman. Their work greatly improved the manuscript, and we are truly grateful for their comments, questions, suggestions, and encouragement.

We also want to thank all of the people over the years who listened to our Monkey Brothers stories and urged us to compile and publish them. We hope they enjoy this book.

Cecilia Berg and Carolyn Farmer were instrumental in helping us produce *The Monkey Brothers Adventures in Thailand*. We are grateful to Cecilia for her careful and insightful editing, which transformed our earliest draft into a cohesive whole. Carolyn handled the design and layout of the book, and she oversaw its production. As always, we are impressed with—and thankful for—her skill and expertise.

We are especially indebted to Patricica Kaufman and Meg Vogel. Pat transcribed DK's journal notes, producing the earliest draft of this book—a herculean task. Meg (www.megvogel.com) kindly allowed us to use a number of her photographs on the front cover. A gifted visual journalist, she was named one of the 30 Under 30 Top Women Photographers in the world in 2018. Meg's work has been recognized by organizations including World Press Photo, the National Edward R. Murrow Awards, National Press Photographers Association, and Associated Press.

Finally, we want to thank the gracious people of Thailand for their warmth, hospitality, and friendliness. They have a way of living life to the fullest, an ethos that virtually ensures adventure.

Author's Note

In February 1996, I took a month-long journey to Thailand. The primary reason for my travel was professional; I was to present a seminar on environmental education at Chiang Mai University (CMU), located in the country's mountainous north. The secondary (but equally important) reason for my trip was to have an old-fashioned adventure with my long-time friend, Mike Burgett, a professor at Oregon State University (OSU). Mike's research on honey bees took him to Thailand for three months each year, and he'd been trying to convince me, for quite some time, to come visit him there.

As I was preparing for my trip, I purchased a small black journal in which to record my experiences and observations. Years later, while paging through that journal, it occurred to me that it could be turned into a book of some sort, something between a travelogue and an adventure novel. Maybe other people might find my experiences in the "Land of Smiles" interesting? I broached the idea with Mike and suggested that we write the book *together*.

Always game for a new project, he agreed. My journal, especially its timeline, sequence of events and observations of people, places and meals, formed the basic framework of *The Monkey Brothers Adventures in Thailand*. But this book is much more than a polished version of my journal, and while it is written from my point-of-view, it is truly a collaborative effort. Mike and I are full and equal co-authors of *The Monkey Brothers Adventures in Thailand*.

Initially, we thought this book was going to be about Thailand and Southeast Asia, a sort of travel novel about the land and the food and the people and the climate and the sights and sounds of this exotic locale. And certainly, there's a great deal of that here. But as Mike and I wrote and revised and wrote some more, we realized *The Monkey Brothers Adventures in Thailand* is really a book about friendship.

So, thanks for coming along on our adventure. We hope you enjoy the journey!

Don Kaufman
Oxford, Ohio
April 2021

Image of the Pa Le Li Buddha, given to me by my Monkey Brothers on March 14th, 1996, shortly before I left Thailand. The image depicts the moment when the Buddha emerged from his long fast, having achieved the enlightenment he sought. Two animals revered in Thai culture lovingly provide the Buddha with physical sustenance: an elephant offers the Buddha water, while a monkey offers him a honeycomb. —DK

Prologue

Outside my window, snow is falling. Twenty minutes ago, the first flakes drifted lazily, dusting the sidewalk and grass, but it's coming down heavier and faster now, one of those rare, windless events when the snow falls straight down. Earth and sky take on the same hues, a monochromatic landscape of whites and grays and silvers.

It's time to go, but I sit a while longer, just looking out my window. For ten years, I've had this same office in Pearson Hall. My desk sits beneath a west-facing window, and I look out across a grassy expanse toward the ice arena and the psychology building. When classes change, a constant stream of students passes by on the sidewalk, crisscrossing the lawn, some rushing, some ambling, all of them going somewhere. But today is a quiet Saturday in mid-February and campus is hushed. It's just after 10:00 am, and most students are probably sleeping in. And with the familiar landscape obscured behind a thick curtain of snow, I'm reminded of a blank canvas.

That familiar landscape is the campus of Miami University (MU), in the small town of Oxford, Ohio. Situated at 39.5° N latitude and 84.7° W longitude, Oxford is best known as the home of MU. Founded in 1809, the university is regarded as a "Public Ivy" and "Cradle of Coaches." I'm a professor at the university, teaching in the Department of Zoology. But tomorrow, when my plane lands in Chiang Mai, Thailand, at 18.7° N latitude and 98.9° E longitude, none of that will matter. I'll just be a traveler, roughly halfway round the world—more than 8,400 miles from home.

I have been invited to give a seminar to the Chiang Mai University (CMU) faculty on solving and preventing environmental problems, topics that are the focus of a college-level environmental science textbook I've co-authored with Cecilia Berg. *The Biosphere: Protecting Our Global Environment* is used in introductory courses for non-science majors, and it's a labor of love that is now thirteen years in the making.

It's strange for me to think about going away in the middle of a semester. I am a teacher, first and foremost, and I have never missed a day of class in my entire career. However, the invitation to present a seminar at a prestigious Thai university is a once-in-a-lifetime opportunity, one with myriad benefits. It will allow me to study, first-hand, environmental and conservation issues in Thailand; to establish relationships with CMU faculty who have similar professional interests; and, potentially, to pave the way for future interactions between MU and CMU faculty and students.

When I first received the seminar invitation, I immediately discussed the possibility with my department chair. He was happy to approve a short leave for me, provided I cover the cost of my substitute without any contribution from the department. One of the four weeks I'll be gone is spring break, so that leaves three weeks to account for; with grants and funding from textbook royalties, I was able to cover the expense of my substitute.

And as for my course, I have everything in order. I glance over the semester schedule in front of me; I have planned each class meeting down to the last detail, with specific content, activities, and discussions. The detailed planning is as much for me as it is for the substitute who will cover my class. Making certain that everything is ready to go is the only way I can feel comfortable leaving my class in someone else's hands.

Once again, I turn my attention to the snow falling outside my window. The seminar is only part of the reason for my trip. I have little or no idea what to expect in Chiang Mai, aside from the fact that my best friend from college will be picking me up at the airport.

Mike Burgett and I have enjoyed a long and enduring friendship. We met in the fall of 1962, when we were both freshman biology majors at Edinboro State Teachers College in Edinboro, Pennsylvania (now Edinboro University of Pennsylvania, or EUP). To the casual observer, we didn't seem to have much in common. Mike was a local, or a townie, as they're called, and I was an urban kid from north Pittsburgh. I was raised Catholic, by a devout mother and an equally spiritual (though non-Catholic) father. My parents were also fairly strict, at least relative to most of my friends' parents. Mike's upbringing was looser, affording him more room to question and explore. I loved sports, especially wrestling and baseball. It's a passion I shared with my dad and younger brother. I even wrestled all four years at Edinboro. Mike never cared about competitive sports, or sports at all, really, though he loved to hunt and fish, and for as long as I've known him, to be out in the woods. He can still hike circles around most people.

It's that love of being outdoors, and a deep appreciation for living things (which, after all, *is* the study of biology), that brought us together. During our undergraduate days,

Mike and I spent a great deal of time mucking around in local wetlands and ponds, taking the Biology Department's pontoon boat out on Edinboro Lake, exploring the dunes of Lake Erie's Presque Isle (an hour or so north of campus), hunting small game, and fishing. After long days outdoors, we'd move indoors at night, discussing topics ranging from politics to women to education to women to the best fishing spots in the area, all over beers or gin-and-tonics. We grew close. Somewhere along the way, he began calling me "Jake," though I can't remember now when that first started or why.

Mike and I graduated from Edinboro in 1966, just as hostilities in Southeast Asia began to heat up. I took a teaching position at Waterford Elementary School and also coached wrestling at nearby Ft. LeBoeuf High School. I started on a master's program at Edinboro. By that time, I was married and had been blessed with two children. For that reason, I would not be drafted into the Army, even though I was required to go through the pre-induction physical back in my hometown of Pittsburgh. Mike, however, was not so fortunate. Two weeks after our graduation from Edinboro, he received a draft notice and reported to Ft. Bragg, NC, for basic training in the summer of 1966. While there, he also tutored other draftees—unofficially—in math, science and language skills, to help them better their odds of succeeding in life. Just another sign that he was born to teach.

By the fall of 1966, Mike's twin brother, Matt, and his older brother, Tony, were already serving in Vietnam. A veterinarian, Tony was assigned to care for guard dogs and Vietnamese farm animals. Matt was a machine gunner on a helicopter—a dangerous assignment that affected him long after his service was over. Given that two of his brothers were already in the war zone, Mike was not sent to Vietnam. Instead, he was assigned to a US Army medical research lab at Ft. Baker in Sausalito, California, where he worked in the entomology section. It was a consequential assignment, because it was there that he developed a passion for research, especially research on insects like mosquitos and flies.

Just before Mike left for the military, we spent an entire day together, mostly fishing and drinking beer. That evening, we ended up at Mike's house, drinking yet another beer, this time with his dad, Gus. Gus was a math teacher at the local high school, a wonderful educator and a devoted family man. He was also a loving father who was soon to have all three of his boys in the military at the same time. The weight of that fact, and the very real (if unspoken) possibility that he might lose two of them in a "conflict" on the other side of the world, showed in his countenance. I was so moved by Gus's obvious concern for his sons that I vowed to myself I would keep in regular contact with him as long as I lived near Edinboro—which I did, until 1970, when my family and I left the area for professional reasons.

Throughout Mike's time in the Army, we saw each other whenever he returned home on leave. We'd hunt or fish and drink a few beers while we solved the problems of the world. During his two-year Army stint, we also kept up a regular correspondence, and I still have every one of his letters. Recently, I re-read them all, and I noticed that in each one, he signed off with some version of "Friend and fellow biologist" or "Friends forever." That constancy brings me great satisfaction, even now, all these decades later. The letters themselves, well, they run the gamut from informative to reflective to flat-out hilarious. In the first, from early July 1966, he tells me that it's late at night and he's just finished a routine of jumping jacks, sit-ups, push-ups, etc. Seems he failed one part of the Army's required physical training—specifically, the grenade toss—so now he's doing extra calisthenics at night to get up to speed. I knew Mike well enough to know that his failure wasn't due to a lack of ability as much as it was a lack of interest. I also knew it was a temporary setback. Once Mike decides to do something, that's it. He'll do it.

Mike's second letter was written while he was sitting on the toilet at 4:00 am. In it, he regales me with stories of Army rules and regulations and more than one larger-than-life Army superior. His keen sense of observation and his wry sense of humor make for terrific reading. Ever the biologist (or ladies' man, take your pick), Mike writes "ovary" rather than "over" at the bottom of the front side of each page of his letter. Nice of him to make sure I won't miss anything.

After Mike served his time in the Army, he was accepted into a masters/PhD program at Cornell University. He began his studies in the summer of 1969, and it was at Cornell that he developed his passion for social insects, particularly honey bees. After earning his PhD, Mike took a faculty position at Oregon State University, where he has been ever since. Mike is an accomplished researcher, teacher, and world-recognized honey bee expert—accepting consultancies in far-off places. One of those places is Chiang Mai University in Northern Thailand. It's through Mike, and his contacts at CMU, that I was invited to present a seminar there.

I pick up his last email and re-read it.

Jake,

Bring some good hiking shoes. You arrive on Sunday (I will be there at the airport) and on Monday we head up into the mountains for some serious climbing and data collection. Sorry that it has to be so soon after your arrival, but the bloom is dictating the work schedule. Oh yeah, bring a good sweater . . . where we are going is 2,000 meters (6,000+ feet) and it will get cool at night. We will provide a sleeping bag and hill tribe porters. Hey, greatest buddy, see you soon. Be ready for one of the greatest adventures of your life.

Burgett

And so, it begins. Tomorrow I go to meet Mike, with an open mind and an open heart. I feel a growing sense of adventure and excitement. Maybe it's that blank canvas I see outside my window. Maybe it's simply that this long-planned journey is about to begin. Either way, I can't help feeling that this trip is going to change my life.

I steal one last glance at the thick curtain of white outside, then pack up my things, put on my coat and gloves, and head out into the snow.

WEEK ONE

When you're young, you think that finishing first means winning, and winning is the only thing that counts. So naturally, everyone wants to win. No one tells you that when you're older, you realize that, more often than not, simply finishing is enough. And finishing in your own way, at your own pace . . . well, that's sheer satisfaction.

Mike and Jake at the summit of the Doi Chiang Dao massif, February 1996.

Sunday, February 18th

I arrive at the Chiang Mai airport at 8:00 am local time. It's 8:00 pm Saturday night in Oxford, Ohio. I've been traveling for thirty-six hours with little sleep, and all I want to do is find Mike and then find a place to crash. Thankfully, I spot him pretty quickly. A tall, thin American with graying beard and salt-and-pepper hair, he's hard to miss among the crowd of Thais and other Asians at the airport. Mike waves and hurries over to where I'm standing. "Jake, Jake!" He wraps me in a bear hug, then just as quickly, grabs one of my bags and makes his way toward the exit.

"We're going to Prachaval's home to meet him and his wife. We'll make a quick stop at my apartment first and you can drop off your luggage. We've decided to head up to the research station today."

It takes my sleep-deprived brain a minute to process this information. Right now? Today? *This day?* All I can think is, no, that's not right, I remember the last email Mike had sent me and I'm sure we're going to the research station, located in the Pa Kia highlands, the day *after* I arrive in Thailand. That would be tomorrow, not today. Today I'm going to sleep. As soon as I can find a place to lie down, I'm going to close my eyes and succumb to overwhelming fatigue. But Mike clearly has other plans. He's halfway to the exit before I shake off my bewilderment and follow.

This is my first hint that plans change with little or no notice here. Thailand will test me. I'm an inveterate planner, a habitual organizer, a maker of lists. It's not that I don't appreciate spontaneity; I do; it's just not in my nature. But since I'm not in charge here, I do my best to adapt. There's no time to shower or change clothes, so I stuff clean jeans, underwear, shirt, and a warm sweater in my backpack, along with other trail necessities. I lace on my hiking boots, and we're out the door. No night's rest for me; we're going to the mountain. For the time being, fumes and adrenaline will have to take the place of sleep.

At Prachaval's home I am greeted warmly. Prachaval is an entomologist at Chiang Mai University (CMU); his specialty is insect toxicology. His wife is a plant breeder who works for the Thai Department of Agriculture. Their home is lovely and quite close to the CMU campus. Within the hour we're joined by Drs. Manas and Niwat, both of whom are also CMU faculty members. Manas is an insect ecologist who did his PhD at Utah State University. Like Prachaval, Niwat is a toxicologist; as an administrator in the College of Agriculture, he is in charge of overall research activities at several of the university's research stations in Northern Thailand. A little while later, a knock on the door announces the arrival of Chumporn, a quiet, seemingly shy entomologist. These four CMU entomologists, along with Mike and me, comprise the group traveling to the highlands.

For transportation, we take two Mitsubishi pickup trucks owned by the College of Agriculture. Typically, the College provides both vehicles and drivers, and a Mr. Boonlut, a skilled driver, is behind the wheel of one of the pickups—something I'm extremely grateful for once I see the narrow, rutted, and often muddy mountain roads we'll travel. Niwat, however, insists on driving the other pickup, which, Mike informs me, is highly unusual. As part of the hierarchy system in Thai culture, faculty are deemed too important, or perhaps too valuable, to be allowed to drive university vehicles and most professors happily accept this situation. Not so Niwat. The trucks comfortably hold two people in the front seat and two more uncomfortably in the back seat. Prachaval, Mike, and I ride with Boonlut; Manas and Chumporn ride with Niwat. We also carry camping gear, food, and water. While the research station is not so distant, the final stretch—more than twelve miles of mountain road—is not conquered easily or quickly. It will be a slow climb.

As the research station manager, Niwat has organized the trip and is responsible for logistics and for our safety. He has an obvious and deep affection for the Pa Kia highlands, specifically for the massif known as Doi Chiang Dao, which translates as the Star City Mountain. Niwat is about my height, 5' 6", and slight of build, but he has leadership written all over him. He's definitely a take-charge sort, and I can't help but notice he carries a revolver holstered on his hip.

I want to add an academic note here. In Thailand, university faculty, as well-educated persons, carry a special title; they are referred to as "Arjarn," an honorific denoting a faculty member in an institution of higher education. So, whenever I mention the given name of a colleague, I *should* write "Arjarn Prachaval," or "Arjarn Manas," or "Arjarn Niwat" etc. And if this were a formal article, I would. But this is not a formal article, and for the sake of brevity and informality, I have chosen to reference individuals by their given names only. My apologies to my Thai colleagues for this American familiarity.

Our destination, known formally as the Pa Kia Highland Agricultural Research Station, is about forty-five miles north and slightly west of Chiang Mai City in the Chiang Dao District of Chiang Mai Province. The station sits on a foothill of the Doi Chiang Dao range, at an elevation of about 5,000 feet. Doi Chiang Dao itself rises another 2,000+ feet, to 7,135 feet. It is one of the highest peaks of the Daen Lao Range on the Thai side of the border with Myanmar (formerly Burma). Part of the Doi Chiang Dao Wildlife Sanctuary, the mountain is home to over three hundred species of birds, including rare species such as the giant nuthatch and Hume's pheasant. I'm told the sight of Doi Chiang Dao from the station is a truly magnificent view.

We head north for some thirty miles to the town of Chiang Dao, which sits at the very foot of the mountain. There, we pick up the road to the research station. But before we begin the steep and winding trek, we stop at a large outdoor market to purchase food and water for our journey.

Niwat, Chumporn, and Boonlut remain behind with the vehicles while Prachaval, Manas, and Mike hop out and head for the line of stalls. Not wanting to miss anything, I follow. I've been to farmers markets and street markets throughout the US, Mexico and Costa Rica, but nothing has prepared me for this. Meats, both raw and cooked, are heaped in piles or hang from rafters overhead; baskets overflow with fresh vegetables of all kinds, many of them unfamiliar to me; fragrant herbs and spices are everywhere; and there are so many varieties of rice that I lose count. Most striking of all is the diverse array of dried edible insects for sale, including ant larvae and pupae, giant water bugs, and bamboo worms. The rise and fall of voices—vendors and shoppers alike questioning, answering, and haggling—is the backdrop for this feast of the senses. Thai village markets are a visual, olfactory and auditory wonder, nearly bordering on sensory overload.

Judging solely by the time and energy my companions spend considering various options, the most important items we buy are bottles of cheap local whiskey and tins of large sardines packed in oil. We also purchase dried beef, pork, and fish; onions; cooking oil; coffee and teas; apples; sticky rice; and hot pepper sauce. Last but not least, Mike throws in a case of Singha beer. We rejoin the others and pile into our trucks.

I realize the market stop is a critical part of the journey, one that involves serious thought and lengthy discussion about what to purchase, how much of each item to buy, and an acceptable price to pay for each item. I reasoned Mike and company must be concerned about budget and weight, since all these supplies must be packed up the mountain, but I was wrong. (Not for the last time.) Mostly, this stop and all that goes with it is part of the enjoyment, the fun experienced by the research team when they are together in the field. I wonder if it's like this all the time with them. It surprises me a little to realize that it feels good, *really good*, to be with Mike, Prachaval, and Manas. I'm beginning to feel a bond, a kinship, forming among us. I'd hoped that would happen, but it's beginning more quickly than I would have expected.

Leaving the town, we begin the tortuous drive up to the station on a mostly-dirt-and-gravel road. It must be nearly impassable in the rainy season. Sometimes we crawl along, and I wonder if we're making any progress at all, and sometimes we reach warp speed, though rarely for more than fifty or one hundred yards at a time. Sometimes we pick our way slowly and carefully through potholes that could swallow a vehicle whole, and sometimes we chug along steadily on stretches of paved roads. And then, inexplicably, we'll happen on a section of concrete roadway complete with rain gutters. These mountains are home to several hill-tribe villages, and occasionally, local governments will provide funding for road improvement, which seems to be undertaken about one hundred yards at a time. Our pickups are constantly bucking sideways, bouncing up and down, and lurching back to front. Overall, it's slow going, but when we hit a stretch of paved road, the gas pedal goes to the floor, and we have a maniacal few minutes to make up for time lost on the unpaved parts. I'm just trying to stay awake with the hope that what's inside of me, stays inside of me, and that none of my internal organs become dislodged.

It takes us about two hours to travel the twelve or so miles from the main highway to the research station. We have traversed the most incredible, twisting, turning, bumpy, narrow, dusty, rearrange-your-kidneys-liver-and-spleen road that I have ever been on, but the moment I step out of the truck I know it has all been worth it. I find myself in a place of spectacular beauty. We are at approximately 5,000 feet, but it's the view, not the altitude, that takes my breath away. Mike warned me that the highlands are often shrouded in fog and mists, but today, the rocky summit of the mountain rises off to the west, a monolith of limestone against a clear blue sky. All of my senses are heightened; I'm struck dumb by the beauty of the sight and the realization that I am here. After forty-five hours of travel, I've finally arrived.

The Pa Kia Highlands Agricultural Research Station sits on a foothill of the mountain itself. There is a cabin with an attached dormitory for visiting faculty and researchers and a separate room for a shower and toilet. Both the outside and much of the inside walls are made of rough-cut lumber; the roof is tin. Electricity is self-generated for about three hours a day in the evening; the rest of the time, there is no electricity.

The station is in an ideal location for Mike and his colleagues to conduct research. Originally built with Australian funding (under the umbrella of highland agriculture development), it is located in the heart of poppy-growing country. The objective of this trip, however, is largely social, not scientific. Our goal for tomorrow is to hike to the summit of the mountain and spend the night there.

The dormitory (also called the staff bungalow) sits a bit downslope on a ridge and affords a fantastic view of the dual peaks of the Doi Chiang Dao massif. It is fronted with a raised deck furnished with tables and benches. Standing on the deck, I feel wrapped in the wind and weather, keenly aware that I am *in* the mountains. The sense of space is overpowering. Light plays on the nearby mountain peaks, skipping from one stone outcropping to another in a mesmerizing dance. I'm not sure how long I stand there, visually devouring the scene spread out before me—changeable, morphing light on unchanging, solid earth.

The station is maintained by Samporn and his wife, Kampong, who live there full-time. We carry all our goods and supplies into the dormitory. By this time, I'm so tired that I simply drop my things in a corner, spread two woven mats, one atop the other, on the floor, make a pillow of my jacket, pull a wool blanket over me, and fall into a deep sleep. When I awake, twelve hours later, I am refreshed. I remember feeling the wind pushing against the station walls during the night. At times, it seemed like the wind pushed *through* the wall—drafty but not in an unpleasant way. I remember going outside twice to feel the wind on my face.

Through the night, I had two dreams. In the first, howling winds rushed down the mountain, tearing at the station. The building stood strong, but as a parting shot, the winds tossed a large limb onto the tin roof with a loud crash. I sensed the mountain was trying to get rid of us—the humans on it—but only half-heartedly. It was as if the mountain understood that ridding itself of humans was impossible. During the second dream, the mountain spoke to me. *"If the researchers want to unlock the secrets of the fields they study, they must ask the mountain's permission to be there."* The mountain, it seemed, had to be consulted. When we leave for the hike to the mountaintop in the morning, I'll be sure to lower my head, raise my folded hands to the prayer position, and bow to the mountain to show my respect. I'll ask that the mountain yield its secrets slowly, so that we can understand.

While I clearly remember my dreams, I have absolutely no recollection of the party—held in my honor—that goes on as I sleep. Normally, bedtime at the station comes early, in part because of the limited electricity and in part because each day begins early. However, this particular evening is an exception. Mike and ten or twelve fellow revelers—researchers, staff, and locals—eat, drink, and make merry while I am knocked out on the floor. They enjoy a leisurely meal, prepared by Kampong, who supplements food she has on hand with the supplies we brought with us. Dinner is washed down with a sufficient amount of alcohol—but not too much, given the need to be up early in the morning—and followed by several hours of conversation, stories, and laughter. Guest of honor or not, I remember nothing. The partiers are too polite to wake me, and I am too exhausted to be woken. In fact, it's probably the best party I attended but don't remember! I know what you're thinking: If you were a college student in the sixties and remember the parties, then you didn't really experience the sixties. I'll leave that topic for another book. . . .

Monday, February 19th

At first light, about 5:00 am, I wake from my twelve-hours-sleep feeling well-rested and ready to make the day's climb to the top of Doi Chiang Dao. In the cool of the morning, in a light fog, I sit outside, waiting for the others to gather for breakfast. As it was the afternoon before, the view is breathtaking and the air is fresh. Behind the cabin stands a great, tall tree, approximately 180 feet tall. Its branches start at about sixty feet, corkscrewing into an irregularly shaped crown. It has no leaves. Behind the tree, layers of green hills, at different elevations, rise up to the twin peaks of Doi Chiang Dao. A light fog partially obscures the far hills. On the hillside to the east of the great tree, eight garden terraces have been carved into the mountain soil. A vibrant array of vegetables grows on each terrace. A barbed wire fence surrounds the gardens. Above the gardens stands the dining hall. What an exquisite view!

At breakfast, I eat a large bowl of a porcupine-and-cabbage soup that Kampong made for last night's dinner. I'm touched by her thoughtfulness in saving some of last night's soup for me to enjoy this morning. It's delicious. I can't remember ever having savored a breakfast more than this one. At the station, meals are taken while sitting on the floor on reed mats. Not the typical breakfast routine for me, but I like it. There's something supremely comfortable about its simplicity and ease.

Over breakfast, I learn that Kampong and Samporn are from the town of Chiang Dao, at the foot of the mountain. They are CMU employees hired to maintain the station and to cook for visiting faculty. In addition to being head cook, Kampong is a skilled huntress; it was her knowledge of the forest that provided the porcupine for our soup. In fact, the meals she prepares for the researchers often include animals she has hunted and shot in the forest near the station. She uses a handmade, single-barrel, muzzle-loading shotgun, taking a variety of birds, porcupines, pangolins, and occasionally a wild boar.

While we're eating, our young Hmong porters arrive: Chai (age fifteen), Ju (sixteen), and Kua (twenty). Hmong men and boys wear traditional black baggy pants with ornate cuffs that fall to mid-calf. They wear western-style shirts but prefer to walk barefoot or in tennis shoes or flip-flops. They are small in stature but well-muscled. Our porters have walked to the research station from their village, San Pa Kia, a distance of four miles. They will each carry forty to fifty pounds of equipment, supplies, etc. on their backs. We pile into our trucks and backtrack down the mountain road about three miles to a fork that leads us to the trailhead where we'll begin our climb. The trailhead is at about 4,500 feet. Our plan is to hike roughly six miles up to the summit, at about 7,200 feet, and make camp to stay overnight. Tomorrow we'll retrace our steps. Boonlut, who has climbed the mountain numerous times in the past, decides to remain at the station. The hike of six miles will take us through, around, and over a variety of habitats. We are at a high enough altitude to experience a pine-and-hardwood mix of forest. And while the ascent doesn't require any true mountaineering skills, it is a constant upward climb, and at times, it's very steep. Because it's February, we're in the middle of the dry season and the lack of rain is evident. The porters hike with ease. These northern mountains are home to numerous hill-tribe peoples. Ethnically, the hill tribes were some of the first inhabitants of this part of Southeast Asia, hailing from what is now China thousands of years ago. China sits to the north of the present geopolitical border of Thailand, Laos, and Vietnam.

At our first rest stop (elevation 4,944 feet), the porters prepare a lunch of dried pork, dried beef, dried salted fish, an apple, and sticky rice with a mild hot pepper sauce. It occurs to me that I now have stinky fish fingers. There are nine of us sitting on the ground in a clearing. When we have eaten and rested, we resume our climb. So far, my legs and heart are holding up their part of our agreement to get me to the top! My boots are comfortable. Good thing I had a chance to break them in properly before this trip. As the day wears on, it's getting warmer and sunnier. I remove my light jacket. The peaks rise above us. We've been steadily climbing for three to four hours, so the pace isn't too bad. The others are aware of my limitations and they've adjusted their speed, so they don't leave me too far behind. Even so, I'm starting to sweat, and as the climb gets steeper, I find myself needing to rest more frequently. Chai, Ju, and Kua pass me, smiling. I am wearing a small backpack, an obvious contrast to their forty-to-fifty-pound loads. I'm the last one in line, but I don't feel inadequate in the least. I'm enjoying this experience, trying to take in everything about this climb—the sights, smells and sounds, even the heat and the aching in certain muscles. I don't want to be anywhere else but right here, right now. I haven't once thought about work, nor have I worried about problems at home. It's good to simply put one foot in front of another, in front of another, in front of another, and just keep moving. Now I'm counting fifty steps at a time, then resting. I'm sweating profusely, but I have no blisters, so that's a good sign. As I rest, I notice lots of evidence that other people have passed this way. There's trash of all kinds discarded on both sides of the trail. I resolve to make sure I pack out what we've brought in.

We reach 6,840 feet in what looks like a good place to set up camp for the night. The idea is to establish camp, then finish the climb to the summit before returning for dinner and our night under the stars. Prachaval, however, doesn't approve. He says this place has bad karma. We go a little farther. We stop and look around. What looks good to me doesn't look good to him. Again, bad karma. (Later, Mike tells me Prachaval didn't like the first three sites because of the presence and odor of human feces. "It smelled like shit," he said, or in phonetic Thai, *kee men.*)

At our fourth site, we stop. Chai, Ju, and Kua begin to set up camp. We're in a little valley between the peaks. I don't think I'll be able to climb to the summit, but I'm not sure anybody else will want to try either. I've struggled to get this far, but I don't regret it. I wouldn't want it any other way. I find my pullover and slip it on over my sweat-soaked shirt. Even though it's sunny, a cool wind has picked up and mists are beginning to move in over us. It's going to be damp tonight. After resting at our campsite for nearly an hour, the others decide to push for the highest peak. What the hell. I take a deep breath and rise to my feet.

It's a steep climb to the top, one that requires lots of scrambling over large boulders and jagged outcroppings—not to mention several crucial assists in the form of others pushing and pulling. The climb takes me back to my childhood; except for my labored breathing and the protests of every muscle in my body, I feel like a kid again, clambering over the rocky Pittsburgh hills with my buddies. It's forty years later and half a world away, but in my mind the present and the past merge; the here-and-now overlaid on memory, their shape and contours lining up perfectly. Men acting like boys, I think, and smile at the thought.

I am the last one of our band to reach the summit, but finally, I crest the final rocky incline and I am there, at over 7,200 feet, atop the highest peak of Doi Chiang Dao. How freeing it is to finish last and still feel as if I've triumphed! When you're young, you think that finishing first means winning, and winning is the only thing that counts. So naturally, everyone wants to win. No one tells you that when you're older, you realize that, more often than not, simply finishing is enough. And finishing in your own way, at your own pace . . . well, that's sheer satisfaction.

We take a few minutes to enjoy the views from the summit. The forest stretches in all directions. It's peaceful here, and quiet, save for the sound of the wind. I gaze to the north and west. Somewhere in that expanse of green, about twenty-five miles away, is the border with Myanmar, or Burma, as it was known when I was young. I think about all the history that's taken place in this region of the world, particularly in the past forty years or so. The remains of the infamous World War II-era Burma Railroad are out there somewhere, long since swallowed by forest. It stretched 258 miles between Ban Pong, Thailand, and Thanbyuzayat, Burma, and completed the rail link between Bangkok, Thailand, and Rangoon, Burma. It was built by the Empire of Japan in 1943 to support its forces in the Burma campaign. More accurately, of course, it was built—in under two years—by forced laborers, including Southeast Asian civilians and Allied troops taken prisoners of war. It is known as the Death Railroad because of the high mortality rates among those forced to hack through the forest, blast through mountain stone, and lay the track. Approximately 90,000 civilian laborers and 12,000 Allied prisoners died building that railroad. My thoughts begin to wander, drifting back in time to the events of World War II and the Pacific Theater. As someone who came of age in the fifties and sixties, my thoughts inevitably turn to later conflicts in this region, particularly the war in Vietnam. France's former colony lies east of our present position in Northern Thailand. I turn and gaze in that direction, thinking of friends and classmates killed in that conflict. So many souls lost, on all sides. And for what?

Mike's voice cuts through the fog of my daydreams. "Jake, you old shit, it's getting late. Time to go." We return to the campsite, where the porters have built a lean-to of found materials. A tarp covers the top and sides; a ground cloth placed inside provides some protection for our packs and sleeping blankets. Kua has started a cooking fire using pieces of dried pine shavings. Loaded with resin, the shavings burn easily and hot. Our dinner, made from purchases at the open-air market, includes sticky rice and beans, packed into bamboo cylinders, then steamed in the fire until ready to eat. Called *khao lam*, it is an excellent mountain food. Accompanying the *khao lam* are dried seasoned pork, beef, and fish. Chumporn creates a masterpiece, a culinary delight, out of the tinned fish with a sauce of Thai hot peppers, onions, and lime juice. The ingredients are chopped and mixed, then eaten with sticky rice and meat using our fingers. Our porters have been carrying water. We make coffee and tea for warmth. The liquids help maintain our fluid intake at the proper levels, ensuring that we don't become dehydrated.

By now, the sun has set and it's getting cooler. The night sky is clear, and a riot of stars appears, so spectacular they might have inspired van Gogh. For the first time in my entire life, I can see, really *see*, the vastness of space and the infinite expanse of stars, planets, galaxies, comets, you name it. I feel small, and at the same time, large. Small, because I am a tiny speck on a larger speck orbiting around a still larger speck in the vastness of space. And large, because I can fit all of what I see in me, in my mind and spirit, and my heart expands with that knowledge. Doesn't get any better than this, I think. And then it does. Out comes the whiskey purchased at the market. The bottle is passed from person to person (the six of us, as the porters have retired), in a ritual I imagine has been taking place for hundreds, maybe thousands, of years. We talk, we joke and most importantly, we laugh, late into the night.

As our conversation rambles, somewhere along the way we discover that we were all born in 1944 (using the calendar of the western world), under the sign of the monkey. Specifically, I'm told, the wood monkey. In Chinese astrology, each year is associated with an element, of which there are five (fire, wood, water, metal, and earth), *and* an animal sign, of which there are twelve (rat, ox, tiger, rabbit, dragon, snake, horse, goat, monkey, rooster, dog, and pig). Animal-element combinations recur every sixty years, and it's believed that people born under different combinations have unique personality characteristics and destinies. Nineteen hundred and forty-four (and more recently, 2004) was the year of the wood monkey, and individuals born under this sign combination are said to be compassionate and always ready to help others; they possess strong self-esteem but are stubborn. We christen ourselves "The Monkey Brothers" and toast our newfound brotherhood.

From the far recesses of my brain, I recall a bit of trivia. Some forty million people were born worldwide in 1944, and six of us are here tonight, sitting together on a mountaintop in Thailand, under a dome of glittering stars, swirling galaxies, shooting stars and random satellites, sharing a bottle of cheap whiskey and a priceless sense of fraternity. Life is good.

Tuesday, February 20th

Sometime before sunrise, I awake shivering. The ground is hard underneath; our campsite is slightly inclined, and I have rolled to the edge of the ground cloth. The fire has died out and I can hear the sounds of my companions sleeping around me. I rummage in my backpack, find my wool sweater and pull it on. I didn't think I would need the sweater, but I'm grateful for it now. It was worth the added weight in my pack. I am warm, and I am content. At this moment, I can't imagine being anywhere else in the world. Mike stirs; he is also an early riser.

We stoke the fire, make coffee, and add some whiskey to our mugs. We talk in whispers, so as not to disturb the others. On this perfect morning, we want everyone to wake on their own schedule. Mike tells me about our Thai companions. Prachaval, he says, is The Fixer; he has an amazing circle of friends and acquaintances at all levels of the social strata. His colleagues have nicknamed him,

Arjarn Jai Dee, which literally means good heart. He is possessed of a willingness to provide help, assistance, and guidance to any of his wide circle of friends. Manas is The Doer. He comes from a humble background but has achieved much in life, largely because of his superior intellect and intense drive. Having done his PhD work at Utah State University and a sabbatical at UC Berkeley, he is a man with a real international outlook. Chumporn is The Quiet One, an unassuming individual who performs well in his teaching role at the university. Mike confides that once, during a home invasion, Chumporn shot and killed a burglar with a well-placed headshot. Niwat is more of a mystery. He's nicknamed Mountain Man for his love of this region and his efforts at overseeing the research station. Although fluent in English, he is somewhat reticent to speak it, unless forced to. I soon learn he's had a good deal of practice with the language: His first wife was an English physician with whom he had two children, and he spent several years in a PhD program at an English university. Like Chumporn, Niwat is quiet and reserved, but he possesses an intellectual sharpness.

I am impressed by the amicable nature of these disparate men and by how well Mike, a foreigner, fits in. I realize from Mike's experiences here that one needs to accept and adapt to Thai cultural standards in order to survive, academically, in the long term. It's a culture that values and rewards hierarchy, and to be successful, one needs a close social network for support and assistance.

The porters add several pieces of wood to our small fire and it begins to crackle and burn more brightly. I hold out my hands, palms forward, to take in its warmth. Before long, the others begin to join us by the fire. Each of us takes foil, wraps some of the leftovers from last night in it, and warms the mixture over the flames. We have hot coffee or tea, supplemented by whiskey to each individual's taste.

Dawn is breaking on what appears to be a sunny, clear, cool day. I go as far away from the campsite as I can, dig a hole in the ground, and squat over it, hoping for my morning constitutional. Nothing happens. My usual traveler's curse. I return to the campsite to find the others preparing for the downward hike. As the porters are breaking camp, I decide to take two large plastic bags to collect and carry out all of the trash we have created—plus what other campers have left behind. I intend to carry it out myself, reasoning I don't have much to carry and it will be mostly downhill. It seems right to leave this special place in better condition than I found it, so I collect enough trash to fill one bag, place it beside my gear and start to fill the second bag. A movement catches my eye and I watch, stunned, as Kua picks up the first bag and proceeds to re-scatter all of the trash. No one said a word, but the implication was clear: The porters aren't going to carry ours or anybody else's discards back down the mountain. Prachaval later explains to me there would be no place to put the trash even if it was packed out—and the porters look forward to packing out less than what they bring in. As we consume water and food, their load gets lighter.

It's not my country. It's not my place to moralize or lecture or dictate ethical behavior. It's a lesson I would learn again, later on our road trip to Southern Thailand. And still . . . I'm reminded of one of my favorite passages by Aldo Leopold—outdoorsman, forester, conservationist, philosopher, educator, and writer. Considered the father of both wildlife ecology and the United States' wilderness system, Leopold was—is—a major influence on my thinking and my teaching. In *A Sand County Almanac*, he wrote:

> *One of the penalties of an ecological education is that one lives alone in a world of wounds. Much of the damage inflicted on land is quite invisible to laymen. An ecologist must either harden his shell and make believe that the consequences of science are none of his business, or he must be the doctor who sees the marks of death in a community that believes itself well and does not want to be told otherwise.*

As is my custom when leaving a special place, I get down on my knees and thank the mountain for its blessing.

The porters set a fast pace. Soon, the others are far ahead of me on the trail. You'd think going downhill would be easier, but I feel the awakening of an old baseball injury in my right knee, and the long-dormant injury hampers my descent. After an hour or more, I'm limping painfully, further slowing my progress. To complicate matters, the trail narrows considerably. There is a sheer drop-off to my right, and if my knee gives out, it's a long way down, so I hug the left side with its dense tangle of vegetation. I hear a noise I can't quite identify, almost like a scratching or rustling in the undergrowth. Whatever it is, it must be close. The hair on the back of my neck stands up. Could it be a predator, stalking me from behind? Tigers used to call this area home. And here I am, the slowest and weakest member of the group, the one most likely to be culled from the herd. Fear rises in my chest and throat, and I realize I am not breathing normally; I remind myself, *breathe*. So, this is what it feels like to be stalked by a predator! If a healthy tiger population still exists in this part of Thailand—which I doubt—I could easily be picked off. I have a visceral realization of the vulnerability of a single life. Then I realize: the scratching sound is being made by my backpack as it brushes against the woody shrubs along the left side of the path. I laugh to myself, and I can feel my whole body relax. Not too much, though. I still must negotiate bends in the path and avoid tumbling down the drop-off to my right. And I have another concern now—my companions are so far ahead of me that I can no longer see anyone. I have to find my way alone. For a moment, I worry that I have lost the trail altogether, then I see the evidence of hikers who have come before me, and I realize that all I need to do is stay in the middle of all the trash and paper waste (both toilet and tissues) scattered at intervals on either side of the trail. I find a sturdy branch to use for a walking stick. The trail is no longer as steep. I'm making good progress when, up ahead, I spot the group waiting for me. They have a little fire going and have boiled water for tea; a porter opens a tin of cookies. It's a welcome reunion. They were never far from me on the trail, I discover, and were constantly watching as I proceeded to catch up. The physical separation was great only in my mind. At that moment, my heart grows larger.

After a short rest, we proceed lower into a beautiful valley where the trail splits. The path to the right leads toward the trailhead; the path to the left, to the research sites, located at about 6,000 feet. Prachaval is concerned about my ability to hike the extra distance to the research sites and then return, and so before taking the trail to the left, he advises me to remain at the fork with Kua. The porter will stay with me until the group returns from collecting data. As I watch the team walk through the valley and back up the mountain on the other side, I wonder how long they will be gone and how Kua and I will get along. He speaks no English and I, no Thai or Hmong. I'm afraid we may be in for a very long day.

I am so preoccupied recording the events of the morning, that it's some time before I realize Kua is watching, fascinated, as I write in my journal. I give him a pen and tear out two journal pages. He draws figures of his family, his wife and two children. His daughter is the eldest. When Kua draws his son, the figure is much smaller; he holds up one finger, indicating the child's age. Kua then draws a picture of a bat and a bat cave where he gathers guano to use as fertilizer for their gardens. I wonder where the cave is. Is it close? I tell him I have five children—a daughter and four sons. He smiles, clearly impressed. I don't bother to explain that two of the five are my biological children from my first marriage; two are the biological children of my wife, Patricia, from her first marriage; and one is our adopted son, a native of Mexico. I skip the explanation, in part, because of the difficulty in communicating such detailed information, and, in larger part, because it doesn't matter to me. Regardless of how it happened, we are family.

We sit on the gear not taken by the other porters, a little off the trail. Time flies. He draws. We interpret his illustrations. We smile. All the while, though, I notice that Kua is ever vigilant. He pays attention to the comings and goings of other hikers. The trail is busy today. I record six groups, three of them bird watchers. Some groups have guides, others seem to be hiking on their own. Most are Japanese students on school break. They are surprised to see Kua and me sitting beside the trail. I notice all of the groups have come along the right-hand trail and they are proceeding to the trail that leads to the mountain peaks. Most have cameras, a water bottle, and fanny packs or day packs; none of them carry gear to camp overnight. I wonder if more and more people hiking to this area will be a good thing? It may be good for Kua and the Hmong, but not so good for the mountain. This beautiful place is going to get busier. I suspect that it may become a classic example of a place that is "loved to death."

Mist begins to cloak the higher elevations, and Kua starts a small fire, once again using his pine shavings. While we drink tea to warm us against the growing chill, he begins another drawing. It's clearly a mountain scene with a narrow path and, some distance away, a terraced garden. I'm intrigued and anxious to "talk" with him about the drawing, but before he has a chance to share it with me, the research team returns. Their trek was successful; they've collected the data they sought. I'm pleased, too; I've enjoyed the hours spent with Kua, buoyed by the connection we've made and our ability to communicate despite the lack of a shared language.

The project Mike and his colleagues have undertaken concerns the opium poppy. Essentially, they want to learn which bee species are the poppy's most significant pollinators. Historically, the mountains of Northern Thailand have been a rich area for poppy cultivation. For more than two decades, the Thai government has promoted alternative cash crops to replace poppy production, with mixed results. By government decree, hill-tribe people are allowed to legally grow small plots of opium for their own use. However, this remote area is dotted with larger plots of opium, far larger than would be used for personal consumption.

We hike the rest of the way to the trailhead, pack up our gear, and at 4:00 pm, we begin the return drive to Chiang Mai. Mike and I arrive at his apartment at 7:30 pm. I doubt I will ever go to the mountain again. I console myself with the thought that I have my memories. And I have the Monkey Brothers. And, as it turns out, the mountain will see me again.

Wednesday, February 21

It's 6:00 am. Time to meet the day. A city-wide power outage forces us to walk down the eight flights of stairs. Maybe the exercise will help to nudge my reluctant intestinal system out of neutral!

Once out on the street, we hop on Mike's 100 cc Honda motorbike, the conveyance of choice when it's just the two of us. Although I've been in the country only a few days, I've realized that motorbikes are the most common form of transportation, at least for students and those living in cities. It's common to see as many as three people riding together on a motorbike designed for one! An exhilarating ride, yes, but the motorbike is not meant for distance travel. We soon join the building traffic and head to breakfast at a small restaurant called Phuket. We order *khao tom moo*, best described as a rice-and-minced-pork gruel flavored with sliced ginger, cilantro, and chopped onions and served piping hot. When we finish eating, we're back on the bike and on our way to Prachaval's office/lab at the university.

Chiang Mai University is about forty years old. It was the first national university to be built outside of metropolitan Bangkok. While Mike works on field data collected on our trip to the mountain, I prepare for my seminar, which I'm scheduled to give this evening. I'm accustomed to the seminar format typical in US universities—forty-five minutes to an hour, with ten to fifteen minutes afterwards for questions—and I'm not sure what to expect given tonight's schedule, which runs roughly from 5:00 to 9:00 pm. But as the morning wears on, I feel increasingly ready. I prepare and rehearse my arguments about the necessity of interdisciplinary problem solving. I know at what point in the talk I'll stress the need to prevent environmental problems. For good measure, I'll throw in a dose of how to properly manage natural resources to prevent or minimize environmental degradation. Several hours later, I have my outline, my examples, my handouts, my notes. Did I say I was ready? The truth is, I wasn't at all prepared for the most unique seminar of my professional career. But that's this evening. . . .

"Jake, let's go. Lunch!" Mike is off; he's halfway through the door before I've risen from the table I'm working at, and as usual, I have to scramble to catch up. I gather my seminar materials, stuff them haphazardly into my briefcase—not my usual way of ending a work session—and hurry after him.

"I want you to meet Dr. Pongthep," Mike explains as we walk to the motorbike. "He was my first master's student from Thailand. Pongthep then went from Oregon State University to complete his PhD at Cornell." Cornell is where Mike did his master's and PhD work, and I know he's incredibly proud to have sent other students there. Mike tells me that after earning his PhD, Pongthep returned to Kasetsart University's branch campus west of Bangkok, where he created an acclaimed program in honey bee management. He consulted on several international bee development projects in Southeast Asia and Indonesia, largely at the behest of the UN Food and

Agriculture Organization, before joining the International Relations program at Kasetsart University.

We enjoy a long lunch, highlighted by a wonderful soup made of ant eggs and pupa, vegetables, and just enough Thai peppers to light up my taste buds and the back of my throat. Since the morning's eight flights of stairs didn't do the trick, maybe the peppers will break the logjam in my large intestine. Afterward, we go to Pongthep's beautiful home for dessert—coffee for Mike and Pongthep, tea for me, and cookies for all of us. Pongthep's wife works in Chiang Mai and helps to manage the family-run chicken egg business. Pongthep commutes to Bangkok, where he has a second home.

As we enjoy our cookies and drinks, Pongthep expresses his concern about the high degree of scientific ignorance among those who make science-related policy decisions. It's a concern I share, one we struggle with in the States as well, and one that will resurface in the discussion during my seminar this evening. He tells me there are no compulsory ecology or environmental courses for biology majors; nor is there any ecology or environmental content included with traditional freshman non-major biological science classes. Again, I share his concerns. Then he surprises me with an impromptu offer: an invitation to go to Bangkok for a book tour to talk about *The Biosphere: Protecting Our Global Environment*. I could talk about how each chapter is structured and the need for changing biology education to include an emphasis on whole organisms and ecology. These are changes we had recently instituted in the introductory zoology courses at Miami University. It's an effective strategy because these are topics students are interested in. It seems like a sincere offer, but unfortunately, my schedule doesn't allow for it. We say our goodbyes to this bright, well-traveled man. I feel grateful for having met him.

We have just enough time to motorbike back to Mike's apartment, freshen up, look over my seminar notes and handouts one last time, and be on our way. I'm to give my seminar, *The Importance of Interdisciplinary Environmental Problem Solving and Prevention*, at a local restaurant. I am used to giving seminars and making formal presentations to academics and non-academics alike and to the give-and-take normally associated with such presentations. I assumed it would be over in an hour or so. We would then eat dinner together, talk awhile, and Mike and I would be on our way.

I could not have been more wrong.

Our seminar starts at 5:00 pm and lasts until 9:00 pm. I quickly realize that there will be no formal presentation, no sharing of notes, no handouts, no question-and-answer session after my talk. Instead, we immediately begin with appetizers and drinks. We introduce ourselves. The participants include Arjarn Anock and another man whose name I do not catch; both are associate deans in the Department of Economics. Lucky for me, the unnamed dean wears a green-and-yellow #2 Packers cap, and mentally, I simply call him Green Bay. The others are Arjarn Chai Wat, a professor in Humanities; Arjarn Manas, Entomology; Arjarn Sumwat, Social Sciences (who clearly suffers from a lack of dental care); an unnamed Arjarn (teacher) from the biomedical staff. And, of course, Mike and me.

We discuss the central role of Buddha and Buddhism to Thai decision-making, the necessity of suffering on Earth as it relates to enlightenment; and the wisdom of traveling the middle path through this life. We talk about the need for interdisciplinary management of environmental projects. I am surprised to learn that at CMU, most of the environmental projects come through the Department of Economics. They put together interdisciplinary teams, but unfortunately, the teams often don't include biologists. Many of the projects concern preserves, forests, and the creation of buffer zones; surveys of the effects of pollution, resource use, and abuse; and the encroachment of humans into preserves and parks. Forestry management (and a lack thereof, in some cases) is an important topic. We discuss how the Minister of Forestry allegedly takes bribes to open up the logging of trees in burned areas—the result of suspected arson fires by loggers. We discuss the complete lack of formal environmental education in Thailand, the abundance of litter and feces on the mountain trails, and a general lack of respect for non-human animals. I ask how all of these things could take place in a society so openly Buddhist? The answer, as I understand it, is this: humans are not perfect, and they frequently fail to live up to the principles by which they purport to live. Even so, they—we—keep trying to get things "right," either in this life or in reincarnated lifetimes. Hopefully, we eventually do. At any rate, we must keep trying.

As the evening wears on, I realize that I am giving my seminar. I present all the points I want to make without once reverting to a formal structure. It is exhilarating. It's also exhausting. It is, to put it mildly, an eye-opening experience. And all the while, we enjoy course after course of delicious food and wonderful Thai spirits. It dawns on me that in Thailand, meals are for much more than sustenance; they are a venue for social exchange and bonding. And for the most part, they are all-male affairs.

Toward the end of the evening, I excuse myself and go to the men's room. Thanks to all the food and drink, my bladder needs emptying. There in the urinal is a layer of crushed ice. Odd. I look at the other urinals. Same thing: a layer of crushed ice in each. And then I realize: Instead of flushing with water, these urinals use ice to do the job. One relieves one's self as usual, and as the ice melts, it carries away the urine, thereby reducing the need for a lot of water to flush after each use. Ingenious! A water conservation project that saves this valuable resource while making money for the entrepreneur who supplies the crushed ice.

At the end of the evening, Manas drops us off at Mike's apartment, where he and I toast the fullness of this unique day. Thankfully, the power is back on.

Thursday, February 22

By 6:15 am, we're up and on our way to Prachaval's lab. We stop at a street restaurant for breakfast—what some might call a "hole in the wall." Eateries like this are found everywhere in Chiang Mai, offering good food at a reasonable price.

Over breakfast, Mike informs me that plans have changed again. We leave tonight, rather than tomorrow morning, for our fishing trip to Southwest Thailand. By now, the change of plans doesn't faze me. It's become the norm, part of the charm of being with Mike in Chiang Mai.

We check in at the lab, but Prachaval hasn't yet arrived. Before I can settle in, though, Mike's on his way out the door. "Jake, let's go! I want to show you a giant honey bee nest and colonies of stingless bees." I know nothing about either species, but I'm intrigued, so off we go. It's a short trip, but we jump on Mike's motorbike and zip to the far western edge of campus, about a half-mile from Prachaval's lab. The area is forested, and the main attraction is a large Buddha tree (*Ficus religiosus*) that has been sanctified; the lower part of its trunk is wrapped in the same cloth as that worn by monks. A small spirit house sits at the base of the tree. Spirit houses reflect traditional animism, still widely practiced throughout Southeast Asia, which holds that places, objects, and creatures all possess a distinct spiritual essence. Animism sees all things—plants and animals, rocks and streams, the elements and earth, even human handiworks—as animated and alive. The bole of the Buddha tree is the perfect habitat for a ground-nesting stingless bee species, locally known as key-tong-nee. At least twenty bee-nest entrance tubes protrude from the base of the tree. Stingless bees are indigenous to tropical and sub-tropical climates and there are about thirty-two known species in Thailand. Mike explains to me that the nests are perennial; the biology and ecology of this group of social bees is vastly understudied. They are smallish bees and have a captivating slow-motion flight. Possessing only a vestigial stinger, the bees bite, rather than sting, as a defense mechanism.

A nearby teak tree has two additional stingless bee species residing in cavities in its lower trunk, but the entrance tubes are quite different from the ones constructed by the bees nesting in the Buddha tree. Mike explains that each species crafts a unique nest entrance form and that taxonomic identification can be made simply by the shape and form of the nest entrance. I am beginning to understand why Mike, as a honey bee specialist, and by default, a social bee aficionado, finds Thailand to be a bee paradise.

Once back on the bike, we motor over to the main building of the Faculty of Humanities where, situated on the fifth-story overhang, is a colony of giant honey bees. What a sight! These bees build a single, exposed comb and cover it with a layer of "curtain" worker bees. Normally, the giant honey bee nests in tall trees high above ground and it's rare to find colonies that can be approached closely. However, the bees also will use man-made structures such as roof overhangs and the ubiquitous water towers. This particular colony is about three feet across and two feet from top to bottom. A constant stream of foraging worker bees exits and returns to the colony. Mike cautions me: We must move slowly and carefully, for the giant honey bee responds ferociously to perceived threats. The locals show great respect to the giant honey bee due to the potential hazard of disturbing a colony.

It's past time for lunch, but I don't want a thing to eat. I'm in distress, plugged up tighter than a bung in a beer barrel. Mike and I have been friends for thirty-four years, but I haven't told him about my constipation—yet. But after nearly seven days without relief, I need help.

"Jake, you dumbass, why didn't you say something days ago? Let's head back to the lab. Manas has a good friend, Prasert. We call him Pharmacy Man. We'll take you to his shop."

We swing by the lab, pick up Manas, take his truck, and head for Prasert's pharmacy. On the way, they tell me about Pharmacy Man. He loves to travel, he loves horses, and he loves women. Mike swears that Prasert loves women so much he has a new sexual encounter every day. Literally. I let this sink in. Three-hundred-and sixty-five different sexual encounters every year. My companions swear that Prasert has never once used a condom and has never contracted a sexually transmitted disease. Okay, I think, this should be interesting.

Prasert is indeed charming and gregarious. He immediately takes a box of pills from a shelf and instructs me about how and when to use them. He tells me I won't need more than four or five, if that many. I take the pills, thank him profusely, and off we go.

Earlier, I was informed by Mike that our fishing trip, which has been in the works since our night on the mountain, is a rather involved and distant adventure. On the return trip to the lab, I begin to learn *how* involved. We're going to a fishing camp on a large reservoir in the south, just west of Bangkok, close to the border with Burma. This is no "hop, skip and a jump away"; we're looking at a sixteen-to-seventeen-hour car trip. Manas is organizing our travels. He's an inveterate fisherman, having honed his skills during his time as a graduate student at Utah State. Nominally, the fishing trip is in Mike's and my honor, but in truth, any excuse for a reunion of the Monkey Brothers—even if it's not the entire group—is okay by me.

Back at the lab, Mike and I grab the motorbike and we're off to his apartment. We spend the rest of the day collecting our gear and supplies and getting ready. We'll be picked up at 11:00 pm to begin our mad dash to the south, our goal being to arrive at the reservoir late Friday afternoon. At 10:00 pm, I take one of the pills Prasert gave me; my plan is to start the medication slowly. I'm hoping it will work its magic and twenty-four hours from now, I'll be feeling much better.

Promptly at 11:00 pm, we begin our journey. As it turns out, Jack Kerouac will have nothing on me this night. Five of us are going. We're taking a Mitsubishi pickup truck, which means one of us will have to ride in the truck bed with the fishing equipment and supplies, as well as a keyboard, two amplifiers, and a microphone. The musical equipment belongs to Oodie, an Elvis Presley impersonator and former schoolmate of Manas. Oodie will be entertaining patrons at the fishing camp on Saturday. He has recently won an Elvis impersonator competition in Chicago, Illinois, and without a doubt, Oodie is one of the most pleasant, happiest, smilingest people I have ever met. The second newcomer to our group is known as the Mayor; he spends half of his year in Chiang Mai and the other half in Chicago. The Mayor is somewhat dour and authoritarian, and he is older than the rest of us by roughly twenty years. Manas, Mike, and Oodie will take turns driving; the Mayor doesn't drive at all and I have no idea where we're going. Because of his age, the Mayor will not take a turn in the truck bed.

We start with Mike driving. Manas is in the front with him; the Mayor and I are in the back seats; and Oodie is in the truck bed. We can hear him singing at the top of his lungs as we go. At roughly 12:30 am, I tell Mike to pull over asap; I *have* to stop. It's the first of four breaks we'll make through the night. Pharmacy Man was wrong; one pill is all I'll need to completely clean me out. At each stop, I have to use a squat toilet. Usually it's one we can find *fast*, and typically, it's outside behind a gas station or store. I take a lot of good-natured kidding. I don't mind at all, because with each stop, I am feeling better and better. My only worry is not to fall back into the pit toilet as I squat over it. It's only after the fourth stop that Manas tells me Pharmacy Man specializes in taking care of horses. Little wonder, then. I had taken a horse laxative. File that under "Things I wish I'd known sooner."

Friday, February 23rd

At 2:30 am, Manas takes over the driving, and I go to the truck bed. Oodie sits next to Manas in the front passenger seat. It's getting chilly, so I crawl under a tarp for warmth. Traveling at 75 miles per hour with only my head sticking outside the tarp (so I can get fresh air), and nestled among Oodie's amps, I hold the microphone and begin singing at the top of my lungs, whatever song comes to mind. We are traveling up and over some sort of high pass. It's getting colder, but I don't mind. I'm feeling so much better now, and I'm having the time of my life. We crest the pass and start down the other side of the range. I never tire of looking at the star-filled sky, and I'm lost in thought and wonder for I-don't-know-how-long, when I realize something isn't quite right. The truck is speeding up, then slowing down, speeding up and slowing down, speeding up and slowing down. Suddenly, it hits me. Manas is falling asleep at the wheel. And everyone else but me is also asleep. The steely grip of panic tightens my throat and chest—we're careening down a mountain at 75 mph or more, and no one can hear me. I jump up and start banging on the roof of the truck cab, hoping to wake Manas and the others, before we crash, or worse, go off the road, over the edge and disappear. *Bodies never to be found*—that's the thought running through my mind. Fortunately, Manas and the others wake in time. Manas pulls to the side, and Oodie takes the wheel. Manas goes to the truck bed, crawls under the tarp, and immediately falls sound asleep. Mike takes the front seat, and I go to the back seat with the Mayor. It takes a while for the beating of my heart to slow and the adrenaline that's flooded my body to abate, but eventually, I fall into a restful (and blessedly uneventful) sleep.

Dawn breaks clear and bright at about 6:45 am. We drive past cities, towns, rice fields being worked by oxen and people, and sculpted topiaries (although I have no idea who sculpted them). Manas and Mike decide that we will eat lunch at a special restaurant in Chanthaburi. I love that name! Also, we will invite a physician friend of Mike and Manas's to join us. Medicine Man, as he is known, meets us at the restaurant. The highlight of the meal is a coconut curry soup and egg noodles. It's hands-down delicious, and with the relief I got last night, my appetite has returned. Medicine Man and his wife have decided to go to the fishing camp with us. Just like that. I am beginning to appreciate the spontaneity of the Thai people.

At 2:30 pm, we leave the main highway to travel another hour and a half down a steep narrow road to the fishing camp. Finally, after an entire night and most of a day's worth of travel, we arrive. The fishing camp is tucked into a protective cove and floats on bamboo mats. All of it. Cabins, restaurant, cooking fires, and eating areas. For nearly two full days, we'll be living on these floating mats.

We waste no time. After seventeen hours on the road, it takes only fifteen or twenty minutes and we're on the water. We use a pontoon boat, and Boa (eighteen years old) is our guide. He is heavyset and friendly. Anytime we snag our lines, Boa dives to free them. Kala (eleven years old) is another "resident" of the fishing camp; he hangs out and, in a way, he has been adopted by the camp community. Fun-loving and helpful, he can spear fish, if we get close enough to the school. Tae (seventeen years old) captains the boat. Serious and capable, he also will spear fish if the opportunity presents itself.

The engine is noisy and powerful. It throws up a rooster tail spray when the prop is lowered into the water. Mike,

Manas, and I are fishing. Oodie, the Mayor, and Dr. and Mrs. Medicine Man are along for the ride. And what a ride it turns out to be. It is a bright, sunny, cloudless day. The breeze is cool, but the sun is hot. It's one of those feel-good days when fishing is nice, but just *being* on the water, soaking in the sun and relishing the breeze, is what's really important. I catch Mike's eye, raise my mug of cold beer, and with a silent toast, thank him for making this all possible.

After several hours on the water, we motor back to camp, where a hearty meal of fish and rice and vegetables, prepared in an enormous wok over an open fire, awaits us. We eat, drink a few more beers, and call it a day.

Saturday, February 24th

By 7:00 am, Mike, Manas, and I are on the water fishing. We motor for a while then float, pushed gently by the morning breeze. We cast and retrieve. The fishing is not great; we catch only two keepers. Once again, I'm not disappointed. As the sun burns off the mist, the lake, the hills that frame it, and the small islands dotted here and there all come into splendid focus. We return to camp for breakfast at 9:30 am. While we eat, the fish we caught are cooked and ready to be taken with us, to be eaten at lunch during the next fishing trip. By 11:00 am, we are back on the pontoon boat. Manas, Mike, and I are joined by a Japanese family on vacation. They don't plan to fish; they are literally along for the ride. Also joining us are Kala, the camp's free-spirited mascot, and the owner of the camp, a policeman in Bangkok. Mike and I learn that Kala does not attend school, even though he clearly wants to and seems to be a bright, curious soul. We offer to pay for his schooling, but the offer is declined. It's not a matter of desire.

It's not a matter of money. The problem, I am told, is that Kala's mother is Thai but his father is Burmese, and therefore, by law, Kala is not entitled to a formal education.

The reality of Kala's predicament hits me like a sucker punch, and I am struck by an awful irony. In decades of teaching, I've seen so many students who gave little or no thought to their education, who saw it as a burden or penance, and who wished, or wasted, it away. Meanwhile, there are kids who would trade places with them in a heartbeat, if only they had the chance. (Note: Though I didn't know it at the time, change was in the air. Less than ten years after my visit, the Thai government ensured access to education for all children living in the country, Thais and non-Thais alike. Problems persist, of course, and some children continue to be marginalized, including those belonging to minority groups, those deemed "stateless," the disabled, and those without proper household documentation. Change, it seems, is rarely as fast or as complete as we would like.)

We fish and motor our way to an island where we will eat lunch. The island has a thick bamboo forest on it. Once we're off the water, I become acutely aware of the heat of the day. To keep us hydrated, we drink a lot of water, supplemented by cold Thai beer. The owner takes his .22 rifle and goes on a hunt for indigenous wild chickens. Southeast Asia is the genetic home (or center of diversity, as scientists call it) of the chicken, scientifically *Gallus gallus*, and it is from this genetic stock that all chickens of the world are derived. Kala spearfishes along the shore. He's quite good at it, and before long, he has enough panfish to add to our meal.

The sounds of rifle shots pierce the air, and we know that chicken also will be served at our noon meal. Tae and

Boa build a small fire for cooking and roast the bodies of the fish on small twigs. The fish heads are seasoned with herbs and spices, then placed in a can with lake water to make soup. After the chicken is gutted and cleaned, it, too, is placed on a stick over the fire and roasted. Its flesh is so dark it's almost black even *before* the meat is roasted. No white meat, no fat, no feathers on the bird! I eat the roasted fish and chicken, and I would try the fish head soup, were it not for the cows on the island and all of the cow dung along the water's edge, right in the spot where they collected the water for the soup. I can't convince myself that the water was boiled long enough to kill any potential pathogens.

As we eat, I admire the view from this beautiful little spot on the water. This reservoir was created about 1964 or so when the Thai government dammed the Kwai River. I wonder, what was the river like before it was dammed? I try to imagine the area without this reservoir, an untamed and free-flowing river cutting through thick, tropical lowland forest. Biologically, a dammed river is a damned river—consigned to a loss of species diversity, a loss of natural habitats within the course of the waterway, and a loss of its intrinsic wildness.

I remember the movie, *The Bridge on the River Kwai*. I've seen this movie at least three times, and each time, I saw it differently. The first time I saw it was when the movie came out in 1957, just a dozen years after the end of World War II. Recent history. I was thirteen, and my family and I saw it at the movie theater. At that age, my friends and I still played a lot of war games, and often as not, our imagined battles were against the Japanese. No doubt, the prevailing anti-Japanese sentiment played a role in our choice of enemies, but an equally significant reason was far more personal. My dad, his brothers and cousins, his friends, and our neighbors all fought in World War II, and many, if not most, fought in the Pacific Theater. When they returned from war, they brought home a wealth of mementos from their time in the military. I had an amazing collection of army patches (each one designed for a different military unit), a regular-issue canteen and belt, an army helmet, a regulation duffel bag in which to carry my supplies and a Japanese flag, the feared and dreaded Rising Sun. My dad's cousin had taken the flag when his unit moved into an abandoned enemy stronghold near the end of the conflict. At thirteen, I looked at World War II as a case of good guys versus bad guys, and so for me, I found the movie's climatic explosion, which brings down the bridge and dooms the train, thrilling. I loved William Holden; I despised Sessue Hayakawa.

Fast-forward to the second time I watched the movie. It was aired as a special television event in the 1960s. By now, I'm in college, and because I'm so wrapped up in the movement against the Vietnam "conflict," I see the movie as an example of the stupidity and folly of war. Many of my friends are serving in the army, including Mike and his two brothers. Watching, I can feel myself becoming upset by the dictum to follow orders blindly, no matter what the consequences. Interestingly, it's a dictum adhered to by both the British commander of the prisoners, played by Alec Guinness, and the POW camp commandant, played by Hayakawa. Despite the mixed feelings the movie arouses, I find that I still love the train-wreck scene.

The third time I watched the movie was sometime in the early 1990s, a few years before my trip to Thailand. Again, I'm struck by the difference in my reaction to it. I look beyond the movie to discern what's real and what's not. I do a little digging and discover that there are numerous historical inaccuracies in the movie. For one thing, the major railway bridge that's described in the novel and film didn't actually cross the river we now call the Kwai. For another, POWs and civilian laborers were treated much more harshly than the film depicts. And finally, the intimation that British officers worked on the bridge willingly, largely to demonstrate their superior efficiency to the Japanese, is incorrect. In his 1962 book, *Through the Valley of the Kwai*, Ernest Gordon, a survivor of the railway construction and the POW camps near it, is adamant that the British never worked on the bridge willingly; they did so only under force (at the point of a bayonet or the end of a bamboo lash) and they tried to sabotage the project whenever they had the chance. Nevertheless, I am interested in the beauty of the place where the movie was shot, which happened to be, at the time of the filming, Ceylon (now Sri Lanka). And I am interested in the nuances of the characters as they interact with one another—and react to the demands and constraints of their situation. I suppose it's a combination of age and experience, but I am a little more sympathetic towards the characters, including the commandants on both sides. They are in untenable positions, and they try to make the best of things. I have come to truly appreciate the skillful acting craft of Guinness and Hayakawa. And I still love the climatic train-wreck scene.

Manas gives the signal that it's time to move on. As I did on the mountain, I gather the trash and leftovers from our meal in plastic garbage bags. And as it was on the mountain, just as we leave, our Thai host takes the bags and empties the trash along the shore and in the vegetation at the water's edge. It's especially disheartening to see the amount of plastic waste left behind. Plastic water bottles, plastic hair clips, plastic food packaging, plastic utensils. It will all be here, same as I see it today, for decades upon decades. Ironically, my mind flashes to the scene in *The Graduate,* when Dustin Hoffman's character, Benjamin, is given career advice by Mr. McGuire, a friend of his father's.

> ***Mr. McGuire:*** *I want to say one word to you. Just one word.*
> ***Benjamin:*** *Yes, sir.*
> ***Mr. McGuire:*** *Are you listening?*
> ***Benjamin:*** *Yes, I am.*
> ***Mr. McGuire:*** *Plastics.*
> ***Benjamin:*** *Exactly how do you mean?*
> ***Mr. McGuire:*** *There's a great future in plastics. . . .*

A world of wounds, I think, and board the boat.

By 4:30 pm, we are eating dinner. All of the discussion centers around Oodie's free concert, which he will give tonight. Apparently, Oodie is a well-known performer. They're expecting a big crowd. I wonder where the concert will take place. Certainly not on the bamboo mats of the floating camp—not if a big crowd is expected.

By 9:00 pm, five back-up musicians have arrived. Oodie has his keyboard front and center on the "stage" set up to the side of the dinner pavilion. His band musicians play Thai oak congas, bamboo flute harmonicas, maracas, tambourines, and electric guitars. The camp guests are seated at small tables in front of the stage. In addition, local residents have come from near and far to take up places on the hillside above the fishing camp. Flickering lights dot the hillsides where the crowd has gathered. This concert is a big deal. Oodie plays a lot of American rock-and-roll tunes, mixed with country and western. He is Elvis Presley, Fats Domino, Hank Williams, and the Righteous Brothers. He also plays traditional Thai music, to the delight of the crowd. The more he plays, the more whiskey he drinks, the more whiskey the band drinks, and the more whiskey we all drink.

At 11:00 pm or so, Oodie invites Mike and me to accompany him on stage. Normally, in a situation like this, I would run as fast as possible in the opposite direction. But there's the matter of all that extra whiskey. . . . So, we don straw peasant hats, and I pick up an unplugged guitar. Mike gets the oak congas and we join him for a tune. I can't remember which song—I blame the whiskey. But I do remember the flash of bulbs, the laughter, and the genuine applause we received for trying. I wonder where all of those photos are?

WEEK TWO

For bait, we're using pieces of cooked cabbage. In my defense, cooked cabbage is not easy to keep on a hook, and "the big fish" I'm after either runs with my bait, steals the cabbage, or breaks my line. Time after time, from late morning until well after noon, the same thing happens. Each time, Manas patiently re-ties my hook. After a while, though, his smile and the sparkle in his eye are a give-away, and I suspect I've been set up.

Manas, circa late 1990s, at the Pa Kia Highland Agricultural Research Station.

Sunday, February 25th

At 1:00 am, my concert watching is over. I head for my cabin. On the way, I take a lot of good-natured ribbing for bowing out so early, but the long day on the water—and the whiskey—have finally caught up with me. I don't know when Mike and the others called it quits, but it was said, with great admiration, that Oodie was still drinking whiskey and playing when the sun came up.

No one in our group makes it to breakfast but we eat a hearty lunch, gather our gear, say our good-byes, and start the return trip to Chiang Mai a little after 11:00 am. At 2:30 pm, after we navigate the steep winding road out of the valley where the fishing camp is located, we stop for a map check, and the gear shift lever comes off! Manas holds it up for all to see. Talk about luck. We can't believe our good fortune. After the long winding climb, we're on flat ground in the parking lot of a Buddhist temple. The Mayor goes to the temple to pray. He offers some incense and gives thanks for our safe passage, while the rest of us discuss our options. No one wants to talk about what might have happened if the lever had come off earlier today, as we climbed the mountain, or worse yet, two nights ago when we went over the mountain pass at 75 mph.

As we're discussing our options (there aren't many), two young boys, about twelve or thirteen years old, approach on a putt-putt moped. They stop to ask if they can be of any assistance. The boys are mechanics! They repair and reattach the gear-shift lever, charge us 200 baht—the equivalent of $8.00—and we are on our way once more, traveling at about 75 mph throughout the rest of the day and into Monday morning. I do the math in my head. We spent one hour on the road for every ninety minutes at the camp! Still, I wouldn't have changed a single moment of this experience. We return to Mike's apartment at 4:30 am. I write my first letter home and turn in.

Monday, February 26th

We are up and moving again by 8:30 am. Mike leaves for his research lab at the University, giving me some much-needed quiet time to process my first week in Thailand. I want nothing more than a few hours to reflect on the events of the past week—particularly our most recent adventure, which has to be the craziest, most intense fishing trip of my life.

I take a shower, then eat a simple breakfast of cereal and fresh fruit. I've found a radio station playing American oldies, and right now, they're featuring a medley of Jim Croce songs. Listening to Jim Croce, I'm reminded of the years I lived alone in a one-room shack on the banks of Four Mile Creek in Southwest Ohio. The shack had no indoor plumbing and precious-little insulation, but it did have, of all things, a bay window! Whenever I had down time—which wasn't all that often, given my heavy teaching load—I spent long periods of time sitting by that window watching the creek flow by not fifty yards away. I'd think about the things that had happened, or were happening, to me, and I'd make sense, as best I could, of life. It was a poor man's therapy session. And now, here I am, twenty years later, and I'm once again looking out a window as I do some serious reflection. The difference is, this window is eight floors above Chiang Mai City in the north of Thailand! Mike's apartment building is about a half-mile east of the main campus of Chiang Mai University, and my view takes in most of southern Chiang Mai. A pleasant breeze blows through the open sliding doors.

There's something special about being alone. I know some people never want to be alone, but I'm not one of them. I'm not afraid of solitude, and there are times when I find it absolutely essential. Don't get me wrong, I enjoy people. I enjoy being social. I certainly have enjoyed the people I've met in Thailand. But I can't function for long periods without time to think, to order the thoughts going through my mind, to save some and disregard others. Alone time is essential for my mental health.

Mike's morning on campus involves consultations with both Prachaval and Manas regarding their pollination project in the mountains to the northwest. They're planning additional trips to the mountains after I return home to Ohio, and they need to organize the logistics for the project.

At 1:00 in the afternoon, Mike and Manas, figuring I've had enough time to myself, pick me up for an afternoon trip to Wat Kua Mong, a nearby Buddhist temple. It's the dry season, the most comfortable time of year to visit Thailand, and yet the day is already very, very warm. When I comment on the heat, Mike laughs. "Jake," he explains, "there are only two seasons in Thailand, hot and dust and hotter and wet."

Wat Kua Mong is home to numerous colonies of giant honey bees, the colonies arranged in a ladder-like fashion on the outside eaves of a stepped roof. Mike informs me that this is the location where Dr. Thomas Seeley, then an assistant professor at Yale, conducted field research that proved the falsehood of Ronald Reagan's claim about "yellow rain." Reagan asserted that the Soviets were involved in chemical warfare along the Cambodian border with Thailand, and he pointed to yellow residue—observed on both rainforest trees and on man-made structures such as the temple—as proof that banned chemical weapons had been used. Dr. Seeley showed that the infamous "yellow rain" was actually the feces of giant honey bees. Eventually, his work was published in the journal *Scientific American*, helping debunk a claim that had done nothing to improve US-Soviet relations. The monks have contacted Mike because the word is out that he studies and reveres this magnificent insect. Mike won't collect any of the colonies because the monks feel that having them at the temple is a harbinger of good fortune. On our way to the temple, we see a giant honey bee colony on the inside support wall of a parking garage. Because of the colony's location, it's impossible to get close, so we simply observe it through binoculars.

Mike informs me the largest nest he has observed was six feet across and four feet top-to-bottom, using probably sixty thousand worker bees! Though giant honey bees normally reside in tall trees, it's obvious that they also use man-made structures. They are aggregate nesters, with multiple colonies residing close to one another, as they are at Wat Kua Mong. This tropical honey bee species is also naturally migratory, and they often return to the same tree (or in the case of the temple, building) year after year.

At the temple, under the watchful eyes of the monks, Mike is able to put a ladder close to a colony. Meticulously, he photographs the bees and their nest and records his observations. He is building a comprehensive understanding of giant honey bee biology, behavior, and ecological importance. He tells me temples are excellent locations to study bees as the monks will not allow the ubiquitous cadres of honey hunters to disturb nests on temple grounds.

While Mike is working with the bees, Manas takes me inside the temple. He wants to show me the magnificent murals located around its central walls. Each mural represents a basic tenet of Buddhism, and as we walk, Manas discusses each one. It's fascinating. I feel as good learning about Buddhism from Manas inside the temple, as I do in learning about giant honey bees from Mike outside! When we finish, Manas joins Mike at the colonies and I wander to the outside back wall of the temple, where I make an astonishing discovery. The electrical junction box has been made by the Square D Company of Oxford, Ohio. I've come all this way to be reminded, once again, how small the world is, and how connected diverse cultures and countries are to one another.

It's getting to be early evening when we bid the monks goodbye. We all agree to stop for a few beers and dinner before returning to the lab to close up for the day. We eat at a rather fancy restaurant about a mile north of campus called Gang Ron (literally, hot curry) a place known for their Northern Thai cuisine. And what a meal it is! Several of the dishes feature insects, including what the Thais call *kai mort*, or ant eggs. Manas informs me that the dish we are served is actually a thin omelet mixed with the larvae and pupae (not the eggs) of the common green weaver ant, a species found throughout Southeast Asia. The adult worker ants of this industrious species take their own larva between their mandibles, and by gently squeezing, cause the larva to exude silk, which the workers use to join leaves to form their nests. Generous amounts of Singha beer accompany our meal. After we've had our fill and made our requisite stop by the lab, Mike and I head back to the apartment. Over a few more beers, we reflect on the specialness of the day.

Tuesday, February 27th

This morning, I head out early to spend some time in the library affiliated with the College of Agriculture, reading current English-language newspapers published out of Bangkok. I'm determined to better understand environmental issues in Thailand. I'll be solo again this morning as Mike has work of his own. He and his colleagues are preoccupied with data entry from the mountain pollination project. They are attempting to quantify and qualify the keystone pollinators of opium, grown almost exclusively by the various hill tribes.

So, what do I discover? Thailand's population is undergoing rapid growth, having doubled between 1961 and 1992. The country's resources are under great pressure, primarily for economic gain, and there is growing concern about the negative effects of pollution on environmental and human health.

Like many peoples around the world, the Thais are increasingly concerned about the need for sustainable development. By that, I mean development that ensures a nation can meet its present needs without compromising the ability of future generations to meet their own needs. In other words, the Thai people are trying to figure out how to manage population growth, prevent the abuse of resources, and reduce and mitigate the effects of pollution. In particular, they are concerned about the exploitation of their forests. They are particularly wary of proposals to change the rules on buying government-owned land, fearing that if forest lands are made available for sale, only the wealthy will be able to purchase them. There is much discussion of illegal logging and land purchase scams. The Thais are weighing the benefits of raising taxes on land purchases to reduce encroachment into forests.

I also learn about an interesting tree removal project. Decades ago, eucalyptus trees were introduced to Southeast Asia from their native Australia. Unfortunately, the trees require a significant amount of water, and since clean water is a valuable resource, the eucalyptus trees are no longer wanted. Eucalyptus-removal projects are being proposed to help with water conservation. I was struck by the similarities to issues and efforts being undertaken to reduce or eliminate unwanted exotic species in the US, in Ohio, and locally (in Oxford), all of which I have been involved with both personally and professionally. I am reminded of the importance of developing, within a particular culture, a land ethic. (Thanks, Aldo Leopold!) An ethical belief that all creatures—plant, animal and microbe—along with their ecological associations (the land) have a right to exist. I believe that we, as humans, must foster a non-destructive, non-proprietary, non-threatening relationship with nature. We must value all creatures, great and small. And we must foster an approach to both science and religion that does the same. If we can bring these two great cultural forces to bear on understanding nature, the human place in it and the interdependence and interconnections of all things on Earth, the stewardship aspect of human-nature interactions will inform our decisions. It's fruitless to talk about sustainability until we agree on the importance of the land/stewardship ethic.

Of the many tenets of Buddhism, an appreciation of the value and worthiness of all living species, seems to have had an impact in Thailand, where something like 95% of the population are Buddhist and there is a religious-based foundation for conservation and protection of the environment. Even so, they still have *lots* of environmental problems, and they don't necessarily respect the Earth—the examples of littering and forest destruction show that.

If education is the process of learning how to live sustainably on Earth, then in the long run, we're going to have to reappraise the human/nature relationship. This can only take place as part of an educational revolution in which the human/nature relationship becomes the central theme. Can we learn to live without destroying the natural world? Can we bring the great religions to this topic in a non-threatening way? Can we bring scientists to this topic in a non-threatening way? More and more, I believe that environmental education is the key. Is this the beginning of a new professional direction for me? Can I use scientific curiosity as a way to understand how nature works as a mainstay of an overall emphasis on helping others through environmental education?

Wow, what a morning in the library. Feels good. I believe I'm charting a new direction for my professional and personal future.

Time to find Mike. I pack up my briefcase and head out into the warm sunshine, making my way across campus toward Mike's lab. Over the many years of our friendship, he and I have often discussed the importance of education and the role we need to assume to be effective communicators and faculty members. His career at Oregon State University has had an arguably narrow focus in the entomological arena of social bees. He has expressed to me his overriding definition of higher education and that is that we, as educators, are responsible for the discovery and dissemination of knowledge. Both basic and applied research have been seminal in his career and that is summarized by his use of the word discovery. New knowledge would sit in a cosmic void were it not effectively disseminated, which he sees as his role as a university instructor. Dissemination is a required activity that takes numerous forms including the formal classroom, extension activities, and last, but certainly, not least, the publication of newly discovered knowledge, i.e., research findings, in peer-reviewed journals.

Mike's voice jolts me out of my musings. "Jake!" In typical Mike fashion, he's waving and calling as he strides my way. "Let's go check out the biggest market in Chiang Mai." It's not so much a suggestion as it is an announcement, and it's fine with me. I could not have a better guide to the wonders and sights of Thailand.

The market is called Gat Luang, which literally means the big market, and it's located on the eastern side of metropolitan Chiang Mai, next to the Mae Ping River. Mike wants me to see the specialized section that sells bee products and to meet a local dealer with whom he's worked for several years now.

It's after 10:00 am when we leave campus on Mike's 100 cc Honda motorbike. In minutes, we arrive at the huge, bustling market, where we park the motorcycle and begin to walk around. I'm enthralled. Everywhere I look, there's something new and unusual to see. Vendors, products, wares—sights, sounds, smells. But Mike takes hold of my elbow and keeps pulling me along; he is a man on a mission. Finally, he stops in a corner of the market, where an older woman sits on a low stool. When she sees Mike, her weathered, wrinkled face breaks out in a wide grin. Mike introduces me to Oui Pan, and I learn she is a farmer's wife from a village a few miles east of Chiang Mai. She sells giant honey bee products to supplement the family's income.

Piled in front of Oui Pan are sections of brood comb from giant honey bee colonies. The brood combs contain mostly older pupae, and the "product" is sold by the kilogram. It is used as a food item; the comb is wrapped in banana leaves and steamed. Oui Pan also sells whiskey bottles filled with *nam pung*, the Thai term for honey. Mike is watching me closely; try as I might, my expression gives me away, and he laughs. It's hard not to be a little put off—to my eye, the quality of the honey is questionable, at best. But Mike explains that all the froth in the bottlenecks is the result of fermentation. It's a sign that the *nam pung* is the real thing.

In addition to her own products, Oui Pan also serves as the middleman for giant honey bee hunters, who harvest products from wild bees. She buys their goods, then redistributes them to the several other bee-product sellers in the market.

After thirty minutes with Oui Pan, we say our goodbyes. As she is the eldest, it is our social obligation to *wai* her. We fold our hands in front of our faces and bow slightly. Then we move on, and this time, we walk slowly around the market. Mike lets me take my time, and I absorb as much as I can of this sensory feast. He explains that the market is divided into areas of specialty. We spend most of our time in the area where insect food products are offered. I learn that Thai cuisine is chock-full of insect foods, some of them offered alive and wiggling. I see a large display of live bamboo worms, and I vow to myself to try them before I leave Thailand. Actually, I vow to try pretty much anything I am offered. When in Rome. . . .

It's late afternoon by the time we leave the market, and we're both starving. Mike promises me I'm in for a treat, and off we go, on foot this time. Minutes later, we arrive at a nondescript vendor's cart. The proprietor, Mike tells me, makes fantastic, out-of-this-world *laab*, a street food common in Northern Thailand. Basically, *laab* is sausage with curry paste, but there is *nothing* basic about this meal. The *laab* is made of finely minced pork. Seasoned and spicy, and dyed red with pork blood, it's served over a bed of crispy fried noodles. The taste is like nothing I have ever had, and I devour my meal.

Sated and happy, we return to the lab, collect our things, and head back to the apartment. I'm so full, I want nothing more than a couple of beers, a place to watch the sunset, and later, a good night's sleep.

Wednesday, February 28th

After leaving the apartment, we start our day at a roadside eatery quite close to the CMU campus. I recognize the place; we ate here last Wednesday. I again have the *khao tom moo*. It's delicious and inexpensive. Afterward, we're off to Prachaval's office/lab, where we discuss a wide range of subjects with him, primarily so I can try to improve my knowledge of the culture and working habits of faculty members in a national university. Before noon, we connect with Manas and are off for lunch at a restaurant famous for frog legs. After lunch, Manas asks if I would be interested in a traditional Thai massage, known as *nuat phaen boran*. I'm a huge fan of massage; it's always done wonders for me when the chronic aches and pains of my days as a wrestler and baseball player (a catcher) rear their ugly heads. "Sure," I say, "I'd love a massage!" And off we go to the central city.

We arrive at a fancy hotel, one frequented by international tourists. Manas leads the way into the bar, and we sit down at a table and begin to drink. Hmmm. After the second or third round, I realize that there is more to this stop than meets the eye. Maybe I'm a slow learner, but I get there eventually, and as I'm nursing my second beer, I get the message, clear and unmistakable, though it's never actually verbalized. In ways that are sometimes subtle and sometimes not—gesturing to various women and asking me if I find them attractive, talking about the positive benefits of regular (and frequent) sex, etc.—Manas explores whether or not I am interested in a massage where sex is an option. I'm not, but I don't want to pass judgement on him, either, so I begin a verbal dance, avoiding the issue he continues to bring up and instead turning the conversation to other topics. Eventually, we finish our beers and Manas stands to leave; I follow. There'll be no massages of any kind today. I'm relieved, but I have a sneaking suspicion that I haven't put the issue to bed, so to speak. Manas is persistent, and from his point-of-view, a visit to a prostitute is a given for any man, Thai or foreigner alike. As it turns out, I am right to be suspicious. This afternoon's adventure is just the first of three encounters where I'm offered the opportunity to be with a prostitute, and my next opportunity will come much sooner than I imagine.

Leaving the hotel, we return to campus and meet up with Mike. I hop on the motorcycle once more, and we zip off to his apartment, where we shower and rest for a bit. At 6:00 in the evening, Manas picks us up and we travel north of the city to meet with a beekeeper. We're looking for hives infested with two species of mites that parasitize honey bee larvae and pupae. The beekeeper generously gives us three brood combs that seem highly infested. Mike needs the combs to share with an Australian film crew that will be arriving in Chiang Mai on the seventh of March. The previous year, Mike had been invited to give several seminars to beekeepers in New South Wales (NSW), Australia. While there, he was contacted by a video team working for the NSW Department of Agriculture. They were interested in producing several films that highlight the hazard of these Asian mite species. Australia is one of the last places on the planet that is free of the mites, and the government has been taking extreme precautions to prevent the emergence of the parasites on the continent. The NSW government agreed to fund an expedition to Thailand so that a film crew could work with Mike to develop several educational videos detailing the harm these mites can do to commercial beekeeping. The goal of our trip this evening is to begin collecting the biological material necessary for those videos.

On our way back to the lab with the infected bee combs, we stop at one of the finer hotels in the city for a cold beer and some snacks. It's an upscale establishment, and, I soon realize, it also has a massage-parlor sideline. The day has been warm, we've been out in the sun a great deal, and the beer tastes refreshing. There are bowls of cashew nuts at the table. I love cashews, and I'm eating more than my share. Manas has found us a table with an unobstructed view of a small, glass-encased room. The curtains are drawn so that we cannot see in. Before long, however, the curtains are opened, and the proprietor invites us to look at the "women behind the glass"—a euphemism for high-priced sex workers.

In Thailand, there are thousands of "women behind the glass." Invariably, they are young (sometimes very young, which is a whole other issue) and beautiful, with enough variety to appeal to just about anyone's taste or desires. Prostitution in Thailand is nothing new; it was first documented in the 1400s, when the Chinese voyager Ma Huan made explicit references to the country's sex trade. Similar references were made by European visitors in the 1600s, including by two Dutchmen, a man named Van Neck and a Gisbert Heeck. Twentieth-century wars significantly increased prostitution in the country, first in World War II, when the Japanese invaded and occupied Thailand, and later, during the Vietnam conflict, when American GIs frequented the country during rest and recuperation leave (more commonly known as R&R). Whatever the reasons, Thailand is one of the most sexually promiscuous countries in the world, and while not all Thai men visit prostitutes, many do, and it seems that most Thais, men and women alike, view it as an acceptable practice.

I knew I would likely be faced with this choice once again. I just didn't expect it to happen so soon. I also know that no matter how many times the opportunity is presented to me, I won't be buying time with any of the women behind the glass. My reasons are complex. This is Thailand; as an outsider and a visitor, I'm not going to pass judgment. But I have no desire to take part. I can't shake the thought that many of those who "work" in the sex trade—in Thailand and elsewhere—aren't truly doing it voluntarily. So many factors, including economic necessity and a lack of other opportunities, compel women into the trade. Human trafficking is part of the issue, too, particularly the trafficking of young teens.

And then there is another, more personal, reason why I won't be visiting with one of "the women behind the glass." I have made promises to my wife, and I intend to keep them.

We are approached for our choice. We decline, finish our beers, and leave. We have bees to take back to the lab for safe keeping. Before my trip is over, I'll return to this hotel. We slip back on campus to Prachaval's lab and put the bee combs in an incubator Mike has cobbled together, then we head back to the apartment for a well-deserved night's sleep.

Thursday, February 29th

It's leap year, and I feel fortunate to have this "extra day" in Thailand. We decide to use it to visit some of the special Buddhist temples located in Chiang Mai City. Our first stop is Wat Umong, a nearly 700-year-old temple located about a half-mile from campus. The temple complex consists of fifteen acres of wooded ground. It boasts a lovely view of Doi Suthep, the mountain that is the backdrop of metropolitan Chiang Mai. It's a peaceful setting, made more so by the freshness of the early morning air. As we walk, we pause to feed the fish, turtles, and ducks that swim in small ponds. "Talking trees" display signs in Thai and English with words of wisdom. One reads, *Marriage is partnership in life*. For me, though, the most interesting features are the ancient tunnels we explore. They contain murals of the Buddha, and replicas of ancient Buddhist sculptures from India, making the connection for me of the relationship between the establishment of the Buddhist religion in India with the movement of Buddhism to Northern Thailand in the thirteenth century. In the caves, we light incense and candles. I think about the people who built these temples. In this same place where I am standing, seven hundred years ago, the earliest believers brought the way of the Middle Path to the Lanna Kingdom of Northern Thailand. I feel small here, but at peace, much like I imagine a mouse might feel when it finds itself in the hollowed-out center of an ancient, living tree. I take it all in—the sights, the smells, the opportunities for reflection and meditation, and the sense of safety and protection.

Next, we visit Wat Chedi Luang, a temple located in the historic center of Chiang Mai. Construction began in the fourteenth century under King Soen Muong Ma, who ordered the temple to be built to enshrine the ashes of his father. Wat Chedi Luang wasn't finished until the mid-fifteenth century. The structure is impressive in its height relative to its base. Surrounding a central column is a tight grouping of finger-like towers, all of which are perched on a series of telescoping bases. The overall effect is of energy projected in a continual upward movement. A replica of the Emerald Buddha, constructed of black jade to commemorate the six hundredth anniversary in 1995, adorns the eastern part of the building.

Although I appreciate the unique construction of Wat Chedi Luang and the beauty of its interior, I don't feel the same spiritual connection here that I felt at Wat Umong. Largely because this temple has become a major tourist attraction. The commercialization of Wat Chedi Luang is unmistakable; the place is swarming with vendors—selling food, bottled water, and religious souvenirs—and visitors from all over the world. For Mike and me, the atmosphere greatly dilutes the religious significance of this magnificent temple. One of the main attractions for Mike is a large dipterocarp tree in front of the main temple building that annually houses several colonies of giant honey bees. For him, the presence of those colonies makes the connections between the bees and Buddhism a strong one.

We leave Chiang Mai City and travel twenty-five miles to the north to visit Wat Baan Den, located two miles east of the town of Mae Tang. Loosely translated, Wat Baan Den means temple of the best village. On our way, we stop for a quick lunch at a noodle shop a mile or so shy of the town, then it's on to the temple.

I've been looking forward to this visit for days. It's the home of a young monk, Kru Baa Tueng, who has been making a name for himself as a respected teacher, a purveyor of wisdom and enlightenment. Since I am constantly in search of both, I hope to visit him with an open mind and heart. The setting is extraordinary, a pastoral backdrop of rice paddies and gently rolling hills. The day is clear with a near-perfect blue sky, which accentuates the cool greenness of the walk to the temple from the parking area. That area teems with construction workers; I can't tell what they're building, but the workers are focused and intent, seemingly mindless of the scores of visitors on their way to see the Kru Baa. We pass a large tree with several stingless bee colonies. Bees are streaming in and out of the tunnels; apparently, they find this day to be a good one for new construction also! As we approach the meeting house, we hear the tinkling and ringing of bells. I assume the difference in sound is due to the size of the bells. When we enter the temple, the Kru Baa is seated on the floor of a raised platform. A line of visitors slowly snakes toward him. As each visitor approaches the Kru Baa, custom dictates that he or she must crawl the last few paces so as to not be higher than the monk.

Because I speak no Thai and the Kru Baa speaks no English, I have a translator moving with me. He will introduce me to the Kru Baa, who will then bless me. I will be permitted to ask him one question. *One question.* Suddenly, I feel nervous, and my anxiety builds the closer I get to the front of the line. What should I ask? I don't want to waste this opportunity on a frivolous question—*What are my lucky numbers? What day is best for a special event? How successful will I be if I make this decision or that decision?* All practical questions, but I don't want to be practical, not with this opportunity. I want to ask something important, something meaningful. Finally, it's my turn to be in the presence of the Kru Baa. The interpreter and I kneel, then crawl forward.

The Kru Baa is young, perhaps in his early twenties. He listens to the introduction and welcomes me with a smile. He asks that I hold out my wrist for a blessing—a blessing to help me maintain balance and harmony in my life. As he chants the blessing, the Kru Baa wraps white string around my right wrist and ties five knots. The five knots represent the five blessings: Good Health, Good Mind, Good Luck, Happiness, and Long Life. He instructs me not to remove the string for at least three days. Silently, I vow to let it disintegrate as it ages on my wrist. I feel good about the ceremony. It has been a mutually respectful act. And now, I realize, it is time to address the Kru Baa. Suddenly, my question comes to me from an ancient Chinese philosopher: "How do we know we know?"

Instantly, I regret my words. Of all the questions I could have asked, why did I ask that one? The Kru Baa doesn't flinch, but when he answers, I see that he changes the question. How do we know we have found wisdom? His answer went something like this: *If you do not become fixated on appearance, taste, smell, touch or voice, you have found wisdom. So then, wisdom comes when worldly concerns are left behind.*

I am still processing his words when I am escorted off the platform. My mind is reeling; I am disappointed with my question. A single thought fills my head: I have missed my opportunity.

It will take me years to realize that the anxiety I felt as I approached the Kru Baa, my overwhelming desire to ask something profound—*that* feeling was a worldly concern. I got so caught up in wanting to ask the perfect question, something that would unlock the mysteries of life, that I couldn't fully enjoy just *being* there, in that particular moment, in that particular place. Call it age, call it maturity, call it whatever you like—these days, I'm less concerned with finding the answers to life's mysteries. I have a feeling they reveal themselves—or not—as we live, when we're ready for them and the time is right. One thing's for certain: If I ever find myself in the Kru Baa's presence again, I'm not going to sweat about what question to ask. Heck, I might not even ask him a question at all.

We have one more temple to visit. Wat Doi Suthep is the grandest, most impressive of all the temples we see today. Located about nine miles from the city center, it affords spectacular views of metropolitan Chiang Mai. The temple takes its name from the high point upon which it rests, about 3,500 feet in elevation. It's a twisting, six-mile drive up to the temple. Buddhists consider Wat Doi Suthep sacred, and visitors and pilgrims throng the parking area at the base of the temple. Thankfully, food and souvenir sales are permitted only at the areas near the parking lot. From there, we climb a stairway comprised of 309 steps to reach the temple grounds. I'm fascinated by the long, sculptured dragons that frame the stairway on either side. The dragons seem to undulate backward as the stairs climb the hill. Each dragon is covered by sculpted scales. After our climb, we remove our shoes as a sign of respect and begin our ascent to the temple itself. A variety of sites—including pagodas, statues, shrines, a museum, and bells—are scattered along our route. Today, we concentrate on the bells, which vary in size, shape, and tone. As we work our way up and around the temple, we strike or ring each bell. If we can ring all of them, it is said to bring good luck. I love bells of all kinds, so this seems like a wonderful opportunity to build on the fortune and blessings of this entire day. We make it to the top, having found and rung every bell. For added favor, we visit each bell on the way back down.

It's been an extraordinary day, and I doubt I can take in much more. Still, Mike insists we stop for a pleasant dinner at a restaurant named Kai Won, which literally means sweet egg. I'm so glad he did. Located on Nimmanhamen Road, an area destined to become a tourist hub, Kai Won will soon attract international visitors in droves. We're fortunate, though. At the time of my visit, the area is still little-known, and there are no tourists when we stop. We eat on the top deck and are rewarded with a magnificent view to the west, the sun setting behind verdant hills. I believe I'm finished visiting temples, but I'm not; two more significant temple experiences are in my future.

Friday, March 1

It's the midpoint of my stay in Thailand. What a pace we've followed so far! Today, we are going to visit a silk factory and a parasol factory. After a morning at the lab, we eat lunch at the Puket Li Kram restaurant across from the CMU gate nearest the Faculty of Agriculture. It's a simple lunch of *koi teo*, which is essentially a noodle soup consumed with both chopsticks and a spoon. The drive to the silk factory takes about twenty-five minutes along what is euphemistically called "the super highway." Our route takes us past what Mike refers to as "the tourist boulevard," an area on the northern fringe of Chiang Mai where arts and crafts shops, often called factories by the Thais, are concentrated. Touristy or not, they have much to offer a newcomer. Our first stop is a silk factory that showcases the production of this most famous of fibers. We see every step, from growing silkworm larvae to the filature of silk from the cocoons. For me, the most fascinating step is watching as the workers unravel the silk strands from the cocoons and then twist them into threads. The tour ends in a silk showroom, where visitors can be fitted for a silk shirt or gown.

Leaving the silk factory, we travel a mile or so up the highway to the town of Bosang, famed for its hand-painted parasols. Our tour begins with the actual papermaking. It moves on to the craft of constructing the wooden foundation for the parasol and then progresses to the application of the paper. The tour concludes with a look at the talented young Thai women (and a few men) who paint floral scenes on the paper.

At the parasol factory, I meet a tattoo artist. I take the brave (for me) step of getting a dragon tattoo on the right pants leg of my blue jeans. It is beautifully drawn, but unfortunately, it lasts only until I wash my jeans—which, thankfully, I don't do until long *after* I return home. I often wish I would have had the dragon tattoo drawn on my skin instead of my jeans.

A bit west of the parasol factory is the small village of San Sai, where Mike knows a Thai family whom he wants me to meet. The father is a rice farmer, the mother an English teacher in a Thai primary school; they have three school-age daughters. Mike met them fourteen years earlier on his first sabbatical leave to CMU. They live in a traditional farmhouse elevated on stilts. What seems odd is the new Volvo station wagon parked in the driveway. A bit opulent for the circumstances, but it turns out that the mother, Kru Sunit, is a businesswoman at heart who runs several enterprises, including a Thai massage school. They are delightful people, and they invite Mike and me for dinner, an invitation we gladly accept. The husband, Khun Samarn, is an accomplished cook, and the highlight of the meal he prepares is his homemade sausage. After a delicious meal and a lovely sunset, we head back to Chiang Mai. It's a good thing we've traded Mike's motorbike for Manas's ancient Fiat, which Mike calls the blue bomb. Manas generously allows us to borrow it whenever we travel far enough that taking the motorbike is a chore.

Saturday, March 2

At 7:00 am sharp, Manas picks us up. After a wonderful breakfast of chicken soup and rice mixed with chicken hearts, we travel north of the city to fish in a man-made pond on land owned by Apichat, also known as Forestry Man. A member of the Faculty of Agriculture at CMU, he specializes in forestry projects. Apichat is a long-time friend of Manas. As we head north, we pass large gardens with rows of tomatoes, peppers, cabbages, and potatoes. Rice is cultivated in the wet fields, and a sweet smell from the residue of harvested sugar cane hangs in the air. Irrigation is critical to the success of all of these crops. We're in the dry season and it will get hotter as the day progresses.

For a short while, we drive behind a truck carrying an elephant. I try to imagine how the elephant gets in and out of the truck bed.

Made from an old gravel pit, the pond is fed by an irrigation canal. When we arrive, workers are in the process of feeding the fish a mixture of pelleted food, cooked cabbage, rice, and any other non-meat food waste. They beat and stir the water with a "fish-calling" pole to attract the fish to feed. With its small waterfalls and pools, the pond has a peaceful feel. Some large catfish are resting at the bottom of one of the pools; Mike tells me they will be given to the Burmese workers to eat. Beehives dot the compound. At this time of year, the bees are making honey primarily from the nectar of the tropical fruit longan, a close relative of litchi. Longan is an abundant source of nectar and responsible for the majority of surplus honey produced in Northern Thailand.

Manas is ready to fish. He loves to fish, as does Mike. It's one of the many things that make their friendship such a strong one. Manas projects a rough exterior but he has his sensitive moments, and he has been kind and considerate towards me. Today is no exception. He gives me the best rod and reel from his collection and directs me to the best place to fish to catch "the big one." Manas ties an eyeless hook to the end of my line. Meanwhile, he gives Mike the worst outfit and directs him to the spot on the shore least likely to catch fish! Clearly, he wants me to be successful. I have never seen nor fished with an eyeless hook; in fact, I had no idea such a hook existed. Where the eye normally is located (on my hook collection back in Oxford) there's nothing but solid, smooth metal. Manas patiently tries to teach me the proper knotting technique, but to no avail! I'll need practice. So, he ties one on for me and continues to do so each time I lose a hook, which I do often. For bait, we're using pieces of cooked cabbage. In my defense, cooked cabbage is not easy to keep on a hook, and "the big fish" I'm after either runs with my bait, steals the cabbage, or breaks my line. Time after time, from late morning until well after noon, the same thing happens. Each time, Manas patiently re-ties my hook. After a while, though, his smile and the sparkle in his eye are a give-away, and I suspect I've been set up. Even so, I don't care. I'm having too much fun. Eventually, I figure out the set-up—and it explains how "the big one" gets away, time after time. Lying well below the water surface is a submerged tree where "the big one" hangs out. Each time I cast my line in the water, the fish ventures from his tree, grabs my offering and, before I can respond, tangles and breaks my line on the tree. I'm sure the fish has been playing this game for years—aided, of course, by uninitiated fishermen.

After hours at the pond, it's time to go. Our day has been one of catch-and-release fishing; we return to the pond all the fish we've caught. Before heading back to the city, we eat a lakeside dinner of barbecued chicken and cold beer. The conversation rambles from friends to professional partnerships to shared experiences. We spend a fair amount of time remembering fishing adventures, including treks Mike and I have taken in Oregon and Manas's experiences trout fishing in Utah.

WEEK THREE

My luck is holding; overhead, the sky is clear, but at the horizon, a patchwork of clouds—wispy cirrus and rounded cumulus—catch and reflect its rays. Fiery reds and oranges soon give way to calmer hues of light peach, faint yellow and a pale green that, strangely enough, is the same shade as a young celery stalk. Before long, these colors yield to dark blues and purples, and soon after, night falls. Stars appear, faint at first but brighter and more intense as the darkness deepens. In that dome of stars, constellations take shape, galaxies swirl, and the occasional meteor blazes—just as they do every minute of every hour of every day.

Prachaval, Jake, Niwat, and Chumporn at the
Pa Kia Highland Agricultural Research Station, March 1996.

Sunday, March 3rd

If there's a typical Sunday in my life, this is definitely not it. Our plans are to visit the Chiang Mai Zoo, wander around the city's famed night bazaar, and end the day at Wat Pra Singh for a special Buddhist celebratory ceremony. After I shower and dress, I head out to the kitchen, and fittingly—for an atypical day—Mike hands me a beer. Not my usual breakfast beverage, but I accept. He explains that this is a "Singha beer morning"—the Thai version of our "Olympia beer omelets." Whenever I visit Mike in Corvallis, we always take off for a two- or three-day fishing trip, and on the morning of our departure, Mike prepares his specialty, an omelet in which he substitutes the favorite-son beverage of Tumwater, Washington, for the usual milk or cream. Tumwater is the site of the original brewery, but it's close to Olympia, and I suppose the founders thought "Olympia Beer" had a nicer ring to it. At any rate, we toast the secret ingredient—"It's the water!"—and eat up. There's no food, I'm afraid, only liquid calories. The beer is warm, and it settles smoothly on my empty stomach, but it travels to my brain in no time at all and leaves me with a pleasant buzz.

We head down to the parking lot of the apartment building and grab a couple of sweet rolls from a street vendor. Mike explains that our host for this morning's zoo visit is a nurse at the CMU teaching hospital. She's an old friend of Manas's; the two of them sing together in a group known as the Old Goat Band. Mike refers to her as the Singing Nurse, but her given name is Pornthawee.

As we wait in the parking lot, I pay more attention to the ubiquitous tables, raised platforms, and ornate spirit houses—most of them paying homage to elephants—that grace the city. Atop one four-foot-high table sits a grouping of nine carved elephants, one large and the others small. They rest on the three-by-four-foot surface, posed to look like a herd milling about the matriarchal leader. All are the same dark teak color. Many smaller, multi-hued elephants are on a dais at least ten feet high. A third, smaller table is loaded with a great pile of elephants, one on top of the other. Used as both beasts of burden and instruments of warfare, elephants have a long connection with Thai culture. Thailand is, of course, in the heart of the homeland of the Asian elephant.

On our way to the zoo, we stop for brunch on the main east-west boulevard of Chiang Mai. The specialty is fried rice, a favorite of mine, and it's delicious. Of course, Mike and I each have a beer. It's getting hotter and it's important for us to maintain our fluid levels. We take our time eating and drinking, and the leisurely meal gives me a chance to become acquainted with the Singing Nurse. She possesses a bright and willing smile—not uncommon in this "Land of Smiles"—and a refreshingly good command of the English language.

We finish our meal and head off to the zoo. I've always had a love-hate relationship with zoos. I realize they play a critical role in the conservation of animals, particularly in breeding endangered species, but I find it distressing to see animals that are exhibited in unnatural or badly maintained enclosures. I needn't have worried. The Chiang Mai Zoo, for the most part, exceeded my expectations.

The zoo is located at the base of Doi Suthep, just west of CMU, and the site encompasses over two hundred partially forested acres. Established in 1977, it was the first commercial zoo in Northern Thailand. Although privately managed, the Chiang Mai Zoo is under the direct patronage of the King of Thailand. That patronage is important.

It is a source of great pride for the people of Chiang Mai *and* a source of financial stability for the zoo, ensuring its longevity. I reason: Since the Chiang Mai Zoo is important to the King, those who manage it will pay extra attention to the animals' welfare and are more likely to provide ethical care and more natural settings for exhibits.

The zoo houses animals from all around the world and boasts a natural tropical forest ecosystem, elegant fountains, and manicured gardens. As visitors walk about the grounds, they are treated to up-close-and-personal interactions with various animals. I can't help but notice that there is ample room for expansion; I envision special exhibits with rare animals from far-off places and some type of air-conditioned overhead tram system to help people get around without using their cars.

Ah yes, cars. Because of the zoo's location and size, not to mention its sometimes-steep paths, walking can be difficult, and thus, cars and bicycles are permitted. Given the heat, many visitors opt to traverse the grounds and view the animals from the comfort of their air-conditioned cars. Not us. In communion with the animals, we will endure the heat and car exhaust. At least the animals don't have to dodge the cars, as we do from time to time.

I'm not familiar with Asian ecosystems, so everywhere I look, I see delightful and novel animals and plants. The zoo has an impressive variety of birds, and we spend most of our time there. The cages and viewing areas are clean and well-kept, but some of them appear to be small and overcrowded. Thankfully, there are no animal odors.

Visitors are invited to touch the elephants, which reach their trunks through the bars to be stroked. To get close, small children perch on the cage bars. Both the elephants and the people are gentle with each other, and I don't see anyone trying to feed the elephants, something that can present real problems.

As the day wears on and the heat and car exhaust build up, I realize we will not have the time or energy to visit the entire zoo. But whenever I visit zoos, museums or nature centers, I pick out one animal or exhibit to see, and there is one special animal I still must visit: the sun bear. Its exhibit is located some distance away, so we get back in our car and drive to the enclosure that houses this signature inhabitant of the vanishing rainforest of Southeast Asia. Blame it on the heat and fatigue, but I am determined to communicate with and learn from the magnificent sun bear.

Sun bears are also known as honey bears. While they eat a wide variety of foods—including roots, insects, and fruits, particularly figs—they seem to *relish* honey and honeycombs. They have long tongues, used for lapping up honey or licking up insects and insect larva. With their powerful front legs and large curved claws, they rip open logs and termite mounds to get at both the adults and larvae. Sun bears are mostly jet black in color. The smallest of bears, they weigh just sixty to one hundred pounds and reach an average length of forty-five to sixty inches. Sun bears are sleek, with a crescent-shaped patch of whitish fur on their chest extending to beneath both sides of their neck and head.

Nature has bequeathed to sun bears two particular gifts. First, they are excellent climbers, with forelimbs that are a little bowlegged. Second, they have a gallbladder full of bile to help digest fats. Paradoxically, these gifts are proving to be daunting handicaps for sun bears in their race for survival. The trees upon which the sun bears depend are disappearing because of large scale deforestation throughout Southeast Asia. Making matters worse, they are illegally hunted, poached in the wild for their gallbladders and bile, which are used in traditional medicines throughout Asia, principally China. The sun bear's gifts have made it vulnerable.

As we approach the exhibit, I wonder, will the sun bear communicate with me? And if she does, what will she say to me? As she lies in the shade, she appears to be sleeping. When I get out of the car to take a closer look, however, she locks eyes with me. Again, blame the heat or exhaustion if you will, but those eyes project sadness. Sad not so much for herself, but for her clan, her species. We remain locked in that gaze for a time. Finally, her lids close and the spell is broken. For the rest of my life, I will remember those sad eyes. I get back in the car, and we leave the zoo in silence.

On our way to the night bazaar (which, oddly enough, begins in the afternoon) we stop at a restaurant. I try to eat but I have no appetite. I can, however, drink a beer. I tell myself I'll find something special to eat at the night bazaar.

A well-known feature of Chiang Mai, the night bazaar is located in the northeast section of the city, quite close to the Mae Ping River. It's composed of about six blocks of street-side stores selling anything and everything. It's always crowded, I'm told, mostly with Thais, but today, there is a sizable tourist presence. Mike buys some handcrafted silk fishing line, which he tells me will be a superb show-and-tell for a lecture he gives on insect products back home at Oregon State University. I buy four small bells to hang on the four corners of the home my wife and I are building a few miles outside Oxford, Ohio. They are well-used and look old to me, and they have bent nails for clappers. I also purchase a carved teakwood spirit guide to attach to my home, to direct evil spirits from the ground to the sky, up and away from the house.

After exploring the night bazaar for several hours, I'm finally hungry enough to eat. We duck into a small restaurant within the confines of the bazaar. Mike asks the cook to prepare something special for me, a hamburger. It *is* special. I haven't had anything resembling a hamburger for weeks. The creation is shaped like a pyramid, starting with the toasted bun bottom, then a large beef patty with condiments and cheese, then a smaller bun with a smaller patty, then a smaller bun with a still-smaller patty topped with a final toasted tiny bun on top. The cook is visibly proud of his masterpiece and smiles broadly when he presents it to me. The burger is playful, fun to eat, my first taste of beef in Thailand, and just what I need.

Following this delightfully surprising Thai-American meal, we head off to Wat Pra Singh. I feel even better as we meet a few of Mike's friends there. We join a throng of several hundred others, and as the twilight deepens, we process around and around the temple. We carry water, lit candles and burning incense, all purchased from the temple monks. Mike explains that we are taking part in a ceremony for the "unbidden" or the "uncalled" ones. This is a national holiday that celebrates a group of monks who come uncalled to the Buddha. Finally, dark falls in earnest, and we are treated to a full moon rising on a balmy Sunday night. At 8:30 pm, we stop to pray and be blessed by a large number of monks. We end our day with a beer and a banana split at the Chiang Mai Hills Hotel, then return to our apartment at 10:30 pm.

Monday, March 4th

After my atypical Sunday, I shouldn't expect a typical Monday. Of course, I'm not sure what typical means anymore. Mike and I linger at the apartment for most of the morning. Mike discusses some possible trips for next week: a fishing trip with Manas; a visit to Myanmar, Laos, or China; or a return trip to the mountain research station. It all sounds good to me, I tell Mike, but inwardly, I know there is something about the mountain that calls to me. In the meantime, there's business to attend to. The Australian video crew will arrive on Wednesday. Mike wants to make sure they find what they need to make their videos. I'm certain he will be a gracious host. This week is shaping up to be a busy one. It'll be interesting to watch how everything gets sorted out.

We take the motor bike to the lab where we meet up with Manas and Prachaval. The four of us drive together to have lunch. Just when I think I have lunches figured out, I realize I don't. We generally have fast lunches. Not today. Today we go to get specials at two different restaurants, both of them small places with limited seating. At the first, we order chicken broth with congealed blood and liver in it. At the second, we order a traditional and seasonal dessert consisting of sliced mango on a sticky rice base, over which is poured a thickened coconut sauce; the entire dish is then sprinkled with sesame seeds. Both specials are delicious, and each is equally filling. After lunch, Manas, Mike, and Prachaval return to the lab where they continue preparing the bee materials for the Aussies.

I'm going to spend a few hours in the Agricultural Library—or so I think. When I walk across campus, though, I find that the library is closed until March 22nd. It's a pleasant day, so I gather as many newspapers as I can find, sit on a bench outside of the library, and read. Activists at the Asian Economic Summit protest the serving of shark fin soup; a potential partnership among Asian and European nations is formed to develop the Mekong Basin; Bangkok-based organizations seek to end child prostitution in Asian tourism; the King of Thailand has launched a project to use grass to stop erosion by stabilizing hills and slopes; and education efforts are underway to combat the drastic rise in AIDS (acquired immunodeficiency syndrome) cases caused by some eleven different strains of the human immunodeficiency virus.

I read on. One story in particular exposes the gut-wrenching sale of two young girls, aged eight and twelve, by their mother and grandmother to an Australian pedophile. The mother and grandmother pleaded poverty as a defense, and the pedophile claimed the girls were purchased as prostitutes, which he argues somehow absolves him of a criminal act. Another story focuses on the efforts of a man named Khun Meechai, a vocal advocate for the widespread use of condoms. Condom Man, as he is known, dresses in a condom costume and provides free condoms to anyone wanting them. As a result of his largely successful campaign, the Thais began to call condoms *meechai*, a nickname that has stuck.

I finish reading and head back to join the others across campus. It'll take me days to mull over what I've read this afternoon. No time to reflect on it now, though, because as soon as I reach the lab, I learn Mike has made plans for us. "Jake, what the hell, have you been at the library this whole time?" Before I can answer, he's grabbed his things and is heading for the door. "Let's go. Manas and I are giving you an overdue tour of the city." I say goodbye to

Prachaval, who's laughing at something Manas has said in Thai, and follow my tour guides back outside.

As we walk to the parking lot, Mike explains that we're taking the blue bomb. Usually, I don't go in for standard tourist activities, but today, I'm game. Besides, I reason, with Manas behind the wheel and Mike co-piloting, it's not likely to be the kind of tour most visitors typically get.

As we drive around the city, Mike explains that Chiang Mai is old, and not just by US standards. It was founded at the tail end of the thirteenth century—ironic, given that the name Chiang Mai translates as "New City" in English. It was established on the site of an older city, Wiang Nopburi, home to the Lawa people, a mountain ethnic group of Northern Thailand. With some 290,000 people in the greater metropolitan area, Chiang Mai is the largest city in Northern Thailand and the second largest (after Bangkok) in the country overall. It's also important historically. That's largely because Chiang Mai is strategically located on the Ping River, a major tributary of the Chao Phraya River, and was situated close to major trading routes in the region. The Chao Phraya is Thailand's largest river, draining the central part of the country as it flows south through Bangkok and into the Gulf of Thailand.

As we drive, it strikes me that Chiang Mai does not have the same kind of big-city feel that you experience in Bangkok, and I ask about its population size. Mike tells me that it's somewhere around one million people, give or take. The mountainous terrain makes it difficult to get a truly accurate census. He also tells me that if you ask ten Thais how big Chiang Mai is, you'll get fifteen different estimates.

At one point, Manas stops the car; he wants to show me something. Here, in the center of this bustling metropolis, is the site of the original city. Manas explains that ancient Chiang Mai was surrounded by a moat and defensive wall, measures meant to protect the people from multiple threats, including the armies of the Mongol empire. We examine a section of that wall, and I realize that it was over four hundred years old by the time the United States of America declared its independence from England! Nothing puts life into perspective better than travel.

We stroll along the wall for a short while, then head back to the car. The official segment of our tour, I soon realize, is now over. We move to a tour customized by Manas and Mike—a Monkey Brothers tour. We drive towards the campus to a street just off Niman Road and stop at an establishment notorious as the oldest brothel in Chiang Mai. Brothels, Manas informs me, are a separate entity from massage parlors. The service is standard with the customer negotiating a price with the woman of choice. Our purpose is to have a beer and to expose me to yet another side of the sex Industry. Our intention is not to do any "business" and we don't.

It's been a full day, and before long, we realize we're famished. Fortunately, Manas knows of a restaurant nearby that he's sure we'll like. He's right. We start off by sharing a large portion of sticky rice, which we eat by the fingers-full, dragging the rice through a spicy dip that features hot Thai chili peppers. My eyes water, and the back of my throat burns, but I can't stop digging in anyway. For the main course, I try fish roasted in banana leaves and served with a spiced fish paste. I'm not sure what kind of fish it is, but it's definitely mild, allowing the taste of banana to infuse the filet. It's absolutely delicious. Mike chooses a pork belly curry, and I try that as well—also tasty, but I prefer the fish. I'm not exactly sure what Manas orders, but he devours it as heartily as Mike and I do. Touring is hungry work. As usual, we cleanse our palates with copious amounts of Singha beer.

After all that food, we're all a little quiet on the return trip to the university, where Mike and I say our good-byes to Manas, hop on the motorbike, and head for home. It's going to feel wonderful to hit the hay tonight.

Tuesday, March 5th

I rest longer and better than I have in weeks, sleeping until well after eight o'clock. I hear Mike up and about, so I get up, grab a cup of coffee, and shower. We're out of the apartment within the hour. After a stop at Dunkin' Donuts for an American-style, carbohydrates-saturated "meal," we go west to Manas's home. Mike then leaves for the lab, where he's busy for most of the day. We plan to meet up at lunch. Meanwhile, Manas and I return to Wat Chedi Luang to pay our respects to one of Manas's old friends, a former member of the Old Goat Band, upon the fiftieth day after his death.

A fortune teller sits inside the temple, and Manas asks if I want to know my fortune. I'm game if he is. I've never had my future told to me before because I don't want to know what's in store. Where's the fun in knowing? I prefer to find out as I live it. But when in Thailand... as the saying goes.

Siam si is the Thai version of a fortune-telling practice that originated in China, where it's known as Kau Chim or Kau Cim. Westerners often refer to it as Chien Tung, or Chinese Fortune Sticks. When it's my turn to approach, I take a moment to absorb the scene. Atop a simple altar is a beautifully painted wooden cabinet with a series of drawers numbered from one to one hundred. In front of the cabinet is a tall cylindrical cup that contains one hundred long bamboo sticks. They look something like incense sticks except they're flat and painted red on the tips. On each stick is written a different number in both Arabic and Chinese. I pay and am told to stir the sticks within the cup, then gently tilt it forward and downward. As I do, several sticks fall out. No good. The attendant instructs me to return the sticks to the cup and repeat the process. This time, a single stick falls out. I pick it up and read, #7. The attendant motions toward the cabinet and I step forward, open drawer #7, and pull out a folded piece of paper with my fortune written on it. It says, "This is the best time of your life. Your family and friends are all good to you. But you yourself are irritated, discontented and restless. Calm down and curb your greed by giving away to the needy. To give is like growing a fruit tree near the house. It will bear fruit in the future. Unexpected fortune is coming your way. Your lost property will be regained. Prospect for love is bright." I get goose bumps. If I'm going to spend the rest of my days living out this fortune, that's alright with me. Cosmic! I read my fortune out loud to Manas. He smiles broadly and says something in Thai. I don't know exactly what he's said, but it's clearly something akin to "Congratulations!" or "Way to go!"

It's Manas's turn now. He pays his money, takes the cup, stirs the sticks, and lets one fall to the floor. He picks it up, looks at the number, and steps forward to open the corresponding drawer and retrieve his fortune. Manas unfolds his paper and reads to himself. As I watch, he becomes visibly upset by what he's reading. Then he does something surprising—something I had never before (or since) seen. He refolds the paper, seeks out the attendant and demands, without additional payment, a different fortune paper. After some animated discussion, he gets one. This time, the fortune is agreeable to him. Manas is once again his happy, smiling self. Without further comment, we leave the temple.

Manas is planning to visit his mother and asks me to come along. Again, I'm game, so off we go.

Manas's mother is eighty-two, and she lives with his auntie. She is suffering from dementia, with hardly any long-term memories to call upon. Manas provides financial support for his auntie to care for his mother. When we drive up, she is sitting on a stool in her front yard. The yard is small and garden-like, with flowers and potted plants. She has a dog, chickens and a myna bird, but the dog is her favorite. She loves the dog and shares her food with him—even, as Manas says, the expensive food.

Watching Manas with his mother, I see a whole new side to him. He is tender, loving, gentle, and respectful. She has a kind, angelic face and strong hands and arms. I ask permission to hold her hands in mine, which he readily gives. We sit, she and I, two strangers communicating through touch, smiles, and our eyes. We don't speak at all, and yet I feel so strongly that we connect at some important, imperceptible level. It's as though time stops for a short interval and I am blessed with this angel's presence. I will never forget her face.

On our way to meet Mike and Pharmacy Man for lunch, I explain to Manas how honored I was to meet his mother. Manas has two conflicting sides to his personality. He can be warm, tender and caring, as he was with his mother, and he can be coarse, cross and matter-of-fact, with a seemingly endless preoccupation with sex and sexual exploits. I like him for his eyes-forward, chest-out approach to life.

Turns out, lunch and dinner will be the worst meals I eat during my entire stay in Thailand.

We start out with fried frog skins for lunch. The skins are whole, and it looks like we're eating the entire frog. Next up is a watery vegetable soup with cut-up pig small intestines and bung muscle in it. For the uninformed, bung refers to the anus of an animal—in this case, the pig anus. Lastly, we are served some kind of raw meat dish, which I don't try. Throughout the meal, we are constantly shooing away flies. Manas eats most of our orders—for all three of us—and later takes the leftovers home. The conversation centers on sexual exploits, with Pharmacy Man regaling us with stories of some of his thousands of intimate encounters.

Back at the lab, I no sooner settle in when Mike informs me of a "drop everything" trip. He has arranged for me to interview the Associate Dean of Science, Dr. Paiboon, Dr. Suwan of the Department of Geography and Social Science, and Dr. Prasam of the Department of Education. Dr. Paiboon gives me a copy of *Toward Sustainable Science: A Buddhist Look at Trends in Scientific Development*. I believe I'm going to love this book. I'm fascinated by the bringing together of religion and science within Buddhist beliefs. I'm discovering there is no separation between the two. Science helps to inform Buddhist decision-making by providing understanding and meaning to mortal life. No conflict. How refreshing!

Drs. Suwan and Prasam and I discuss undergraduate education, human ecology, and nature study. They are also interested in helping high school teachers get more ecology into their curricula. They tell me about their children's forestry program; children plant trees to improve the environment and to help Thailand with reforestation. They are doing environmental education with children by providing youth camping experiences, nature walks, and nature study tours. They suggest a collaboration. We could develop a joint project for high school and grade school teachers and students from both rural and urban areas. I could return as a visiting professor in the Graduate School.

We pass a pleasant afternoon discussing topics of mutual personal and professional interest. In learning about environmental education within a Buddhist culture, I am fulfilling a major goal for this trip. And even though he doesn't share my professional goals, Mike is doing everything he can to help me have a successful visit. I'm grateful for his friendship and support.

I walk back to the lab, just in time to head out for dinner. We go to another of Manas's favorite restaurants. With his choice of eateries, he's educating me on Northern Thai cuisine. I'm trying to eat everything put in front of me, but at dinner, I again find it hard to do.

We make our own soup for dinner. The restaurant provides us with hot pots, heated by Sterno canisters. We order the ingredients for our soup from picture menus, just as we did at lunch. The photographs of the uncooked pig's heart, raw liver, intestines (large and small), and bung; fish stomach and intestines; tripe (cow's stomach); and jellyfish are unsettling. What really kills my appetite, however, is the visual of the raw ingredients as I place them into the broth. I try. I really do. I just cannot prepare and eat this soup. Manas takes pity on me, and he orders some "safe" pieces of beef, fish, pork, and eggs.

I'm afraid the damage has been done. I have very little appetite. I eat what I can, as do Mike and Pharmacy Man. Per usual, Manas dines with relish and takes home the leftovers.

On the way back to our apartment, Mike looks at me and smiles. "Jake, tomorrow we go back to the mountain!"

Wednesday, March 6th

At 7:00 am, we leave for a return trip to the mountain research station. This time around, I'm in much better physical and mental shape, and I've been looking forward to this trip ever since Mike mentioned it a week ago. At the last minute, it's decided that Mike will stay back to prepare for the Australian team's visit. He'll pick them up at the Chiang Mai airport tomorrow morning. So that means I'll be going with the remaining members of the research team—Prachaval, Niwat, and Chumporn.

We stop for groceries and other supplies in the town of Mae Taeng, about twenty miles north of metropolitan Chiang Mai. As we stroll through the market, many of the vendors turn and stare. Clearly, I'm an oddity here. I suspect the main attraction is my prematurely white beard. No matter. We take our time, finding just the right staples for the trip.

The mountain road is even more difficult than I remember from our previous journey, but Niwat is an excellent driver. As we climb, we pass through several ecosystems. In the top third of the trek, we pass through a coniferous zone. It seems odd to see banana trees growing underneath a crown of pines. This trip, I notice several additional sections of road that are paved and finished with gutters. I must have missed them as we made our way up the mountain the first time. They are seemingly in the middle of nowhere. Prachaval explains that during the wet season, the road is treacherous at best, and impassable at worst, and so the locals chip in to buy the cement needed to pave particularly hazardous sections. I wonder, if there's enough political pressure from village communities, will the entire road be paved eventually? On the positive side, both the locals and the researchers would find it easier to travel between Chiang Mai and the mountain. On the negative side, easy access to the mountain could dramatically increase tourism—and with the tourists would likely come increased environmental impacts, especially more vehicles, pollution, and littering.

At an altitude of about a mile high, we reach the research station, but we don't stop; instead, we proceed directly to the research site. I'm amazed to discover that this road is even more difficult than the one up the mountain. At one point, I look out the window and all I can see is air! It looks like we're going to drive right off the side of the mountain. Turns out, we are following an actual road—of sorts—and Niwat negotiates it with ease. Thank you, Brother Niwat! We park the car on a pull-out and hike to several different sites.

All of the team's research sites are on steep slopes, and the trails to them are difficult. The Hmong grow various crops on slopes adjoining the research sites. They've built terraces into the steep side of the hills and planted them with cabbages and lettuces. To water their crops, they've strung together long lengths of garden hoses that are fed by gravity from catchment pools higher up on the mountain. The soil looks loose and loamy, rich and fertile. I can't tell how deep it is. I wonder, if a hard rain falls, will the steepness of the slopes cause the water to carry away the soil? I saw just one individual tending the Hmong gardens that day—a lone Hmong woman, about eighteen years old. She had a baby, not more than a year old, strapped to her back. She must have walked from her village, about four miles away, to get to the fields.

My companions begin collecting data, which involves observing floral density and cataloging bee visitors—of which there are many. Mike has told me that the native background environmental bee density is very high relative to temperate North America. In this particular high-altitude zone, we see bumble bees, numerous species of the social stingless bees and the ever-present eastern honey bee, which is the closest genetic relative to the common honey bee of North America. There are giant honey bees and dwarf honey bees as well. It's clear why Mike, as a bee specialist, is enthralled with this bee-rich part of the world.

After my companions have collected data from the various sites, we drive to the nearest Hmong village, San Pa Kia, for snacks and a cold beer. The village is built around and up the mountain sides in all four compass directions and is at a crossroads, of sorts. As we near the village, I see a Christian church. Apparently, hill tribe ethnic groups are one of the few successes of the evangelical zeal exhibited by foreign missionaries. Entering the heart of San Pa Kia, I see a moving current of chickens, pigs, dogs, children and adults, all seeming to exist in free-form movement. Most of the adults are older women; the men and younger women, I assume, are off working at this time of day. At the main crossroads in town, we stop at the San Pa Kia General Store. It offers cooked food, beer, trinkets, and processed food. Cooked food is dispensed in plastic bags, along with little packages of sweets and frozen sugar water, as treats for children. There are no local crafts for sale. San Pa Kia does not look prosperous, with two notable exceptions: the owner of the general store and the local drug dealer.

The average lifespan for the Hmong is forty years old. The local drug dealer, Tiger, is also a tribal elder and the town mayor. He is in his thirties. Compared to the rest of the Hmong around me today, Tiger is friendly, and he looks well fed. He runs an opium den, offering a hit of opium at 25¢ per inhale. I'm told he has a thriving business from European travelers. He offers me opium, marijuana, or hashish. No problem! I decline.

I'm happy to see a school here, and I'm pleasantly surprised to find that it seems to be the sturdiest, most well-built building in the village. Prachaval tells me the school and its teacher are part of the Royal Education Plan for Thailand. The teacher is Thai and is working off a school debt. When the debt has been repaid, the teacher will most likely transfer, to be replaced by another teacher with a school debt to repay. With the exception of nursing babies, the children are filthy, thanks to the dust and dirt they are playing in. Mange and head lice are common afflictions among the young. Essentially, the village has no medical services.

Two little boys are hanging around me, playing with homemade toys of carved wood with some sort of plastic doodads attached to the wood. Quite the combination. I estimate the boys to be about seven and ten years old. The older boy is blind in his left eye. Both of his eyes wander; he appears to have no control of his eye movement at all. The younger boy is fascinated by my appearance. I play the "which hand is the coin in?" guessing game with them. After a while, they both guess correctly; they are delighted and immediately take their winnings to the general store to buy a frozen sugar-water treat.

The store owner is young, in her early twenties. Her name is Narare and she is from another hill tribe ethnic group, the Lahu, one of seven such groups. Her home village is about eight miles away on another side of the mountain. Mike tells me that her husband is from the lowlands, and he has installed her in San Pa Kia to run his store. She is very attractive and healthy-looking, and she has two babies. She smiles constantly and obviously has known Niwat and Prachaval for quite a while. We get our cold beers. I ask for the bathroom and am directed to a side door that opens into a small room with outhouse-like seats. When I look through the latrine "hole," I see pigs penned below. What an interesting way to recycle feces. I make a mental note *not* to eat any of the pickled pork kept in large glass jars on the store's shelves.

We return to the research station for dinner. This visit, the canned fish has been rendered inedible for me by a copious addition of Thai peppers. I don't go hungry, though, thanks to the snacks and beer we bought at the San Pa Kia General Store. Prachaval has decided, at the last minute, that we will spend the night. Fine with me. Sitting outside on the deck of the staff bungalow, I take time to enjoy the mountain.

Positioned just-so on the hillside, the bungalow affords a million-dollar view of the twin peaks of Doi Chiang Dao. I can see why my CMU colleagues come here to find refuge away from the metropolitan clamor of the city. The station is a wonderfully serene place; sitting here, stress and worry subside, replaced by a genuine sense of peace. I have a front row seat as the sun slips below the mountain. My luck is holding; overhead, the sky is clear, but at the horizon, a patchwork of clouds—wispy cirrus and rounded cumulus—catch and reflect its rays. Fiery reds and oranges soon give way to calmer hues of light peach, faint yellow and a pale green that, strangely enough, is the same shade as a young celery stalk. Before long, these colors yield to dark blues and purples, and soon after, night falls. Stars appear, faint at first but brighter and more intense as the darkness deepens. In that dome of stars, constellations take shape, galaxies swirl, and the occasional meteor blazes—just as they do every minute of every hour of every day. The beauty of the night sky is impossible to capture in words. I stay as long I can, until the chilly night air drives me indoors.

Thursday, March 7th

Waking at first light, I don my sweater, grab a cup of coffee, go outside, and sit out on the deck. A purple haze has settled in the mountain valleys. No kidding, Jimi Hendrix is playing in my head. I watch the morning routine of the "cut-eared dog" as he thoughtfully sniffs at various spots and objects. One of the many dogs that inhabit the research station, he has a shortened tail and an ear with a defined notch—both, I'm afraid, the consequences of attempting to snatch morsels from Kampong's kitchen. Clearly, she is as adept with sharpened blades as she is with her shotgun.

Speaking of Kampong, it isn't long before she beckons me inside. She has prepared a hearty breakfast for us: fried rice, scrambled eggs with thin-sliced pork, and a third dish of pork and cabbage. Breakfast in Thailand has become my favorite meal of the day. I eat a lot of the rice and cabbage, breaking the pork into small pieces with my spoon and fork. I am trying to eat more vegetables and less meat.

After breakfast, we collect our gear, pack it into the truck, and are about to leave when one of our Thai porters brings us a gift of a special tree bark. He explains that when boiled into a tea and taken before making love, the bark allows one to have sex ten times a night. Hmmm. For some reason, the return trip seemed much quicker. I suspect we are all thinking about the possibilities. . . .

By 9:30 am, we're back at the lab, awaiting the arrival of Mike and the Australian film makers. The Australians are from the New South Wales Department of Agriculture and have come to make videos featuring honey bee parasitic mites, which threaten to invade Australia via the Cape York peninsula in the country's northeast. A year back, Mike had been invited to Australia to give several seminars on the hazards of Asian honey bee parasitic brood mites. While he was there, the New South Wales Department of Agriculture approached him about the possibility of sending a film team the next time he was at CMU. He readily agreed. Prior to their arrival, Mike assembled the necessary bee material for them to film. A little after 11:00 am, Mike and his guests arrive burdened with their camera equipment and eager for lunch. So off we go, to yet another hole-in-the-wall restaurant, one particularly favored by Manas. Mike tells me that he's eaten here numerous times, and he calls it the "tastes-not-so-good" restaurant, which proves entirely false. The Australians, Bruce and Phil, are so impressed with the place they ask permission to make some videos in the kitchen, which Manas graciously arranges. We spend the remainder of the afternoon at the lab, discussing honey bee biology, the life histories of the mites, and how to get the best video perspectives. Late in the day, Prachaval escorts Bruce and Phil to their hotel, just minutes from campus. It is the renowned Chiang Mai

Phucome—renowned in the sense that the hotel has one of the higher-class massage parlors associated with it.

Mike and I retire to his apartment and later enjoy a quiet dinner at the Solao restaurant, an easy walk from his place. It specializes in food from Eastern Thailand, which is reputed to be rather spicy, but I'm beginning to think all Thai regional cuisines make that claim. They have great chicken wings, which, coupled with sticky rice, make for an extremely satisfying dinner. Along with a couple of beers, I'm ready for a good night's sleep. Hard to believe I spent the previous night on the mountain. Seems worlds away.

Friday, March 8th

We get to the lab early today. Soon Bruce and Phil arrive. They've brought beer, which we start on. I have a strong feeling this is going to be a "food and drink" day. What the hell, in for a penny, in for a pound. After a few beers, we're off to go fishing at the Mae Ngat Reservoir, about twenty miles north of town. It's a major impoundment of the Ping River and one of Manas's favorite fishing spots for giant snakehead fish. Mike tells me the giant snakehead, like the tropical pike, is a hard fighter once struck. We fish until noon, then eat lunch at a local restaurant—with a few beers, of course. Then it's back to fishing. Anawat, a friend of Mike's and Manas's, shows up with Saki, a local brew. Anawat did his PhD in horticulture at OSU, which is where Mike first met him. He works in Bangkok but escapes often to the north to refresh himself. He is also fond of fishing. I try to pace myself, making my beer last a long time, sipping my Saki. My pace keeps me upright and I thoroughly enjoy the day. But we're not finished. It's out for dinner at the Gang Ron restaurant, famous for its Northern Thai food, including ant pupae and bamboo worms. Time and time again during my visit, I'm reminded that the consumption of insects is more prevalent in Thailand than anywhere else in the world. Our company includes Manas, Anawat, Bruce, and Phil. The dinner is long and good and very filling. And overly blessed with Singha.

We return, by cab, to Mike's apartment. It's a good thing none of us is driving. It's late, and all I want to do is sleep. I need some time to recover. Manas is picking me up at 6:00 am to go to the morning food market.

Saturday, March 9th

Before first light, I'm waiting for Manas outside of our apartment building. I wear a light pullover jacket to protect me from the early morning chill. It doesn't take long to get to the morning food market, but already, lots of people are here. It's hard to know where to look first. Foods of every type—vegetables, meats, fishes (both alive and dead), insects, spices, oils, sauces, and specialty items like ant eggs and cricket and bee larva—are on display. Between the seemingly endless variety of things to eat, the sounds of bartering, and the competing smells—the fragrance of aromatic spices clashes with the odor of sour fish water—I'm suffering sensory overload. Manas, as usual, walks at a fast pace. I try to keep up with him, but at the same time, I want to take it all in. All the while, I'm trying not to slip on the dusty floors, step on anything that's laid out for inspection and sale, or walk into anyone buying, selling, carrying, loading, staring, tasting, or examining.

Manas purchases giant honey bee combs with larval bees inside the combs. He'll take them back to the lab to look for mites. He also buys a large fish, then has it scaled and the entrails removed. He will prepare it whole—with the head on—for his family dinner. Manas also purchases ripe mangos, what he calls "old style" black sticky rice (already cooked), and fresh sweet coconut milk to put over the rice and mango for breakfast.

Manas offers me fried cow skin. It reminds me of fried greasy noodles—except it isn't noodles. Not very appetizing. Manas, however, seems to relish it. I could spend hours in this place, but Manas has what he came for, so it's time to leave. On our way out, a large live fish flops out of its container, splashing fish water on my pants, shoes, and shirt. Everybody around me gets a good laugh, including me. But now I need a shower and a change of clothes, so Manas drops me off at the apartment. Mike is already at the lab, so after I clean up, I decide to walk there. It's a beautiful morning. Nobody in Chiang Mai walks, it seems, but I enjoy the craziness of the streets from a sidewalk perspective.

It's almost 8:00 am when I arrive at the lab, where Bruce and Phil are filming the search for *Varroa* mites. A serious problem for the imported western honey bee, *Varroa* mites are the hazard of greatest concern for Australian beekeeping. *Varroa* is native to Southeast Asia and normally attacks only the brood of the eastern hive bee *Apis cerana* but following some large-scale introductions of the western honey bee to Thailand in the early 1980s, the mites easily made the switch to this alternative host. We don't find any *Varroa* mites in this batch of bee larva, but we do find *Tropilaelaps*, a mite that parasitizes the brood combs of the giant honey bee. It's also of interest to the Aussies since it, too, is capable of switching hosts and infesting the western honey bee. For keepers of the Thai western honey bee, the *Tropilaelaps* mite is a far greater problem than *Varroa*.

By 10:00 am, we are off to the Thai Healthy Products Company to film the extraction of honey. The company was started in 1974 by Phaothai na Ayutthaya and his partner, Mr. Sungwan, with four honey bee hives. (Phaothai's surname, na Ayutthaya, indicates he is a descendant of royal blood, but then again, considering the historical prevalence of polygamy, so are a significant number of Thais.) Business is booming, Mike tells me. (So much so, that in ten years' time, by 2006, the company had 5,000 hives and was a $2 million/year operation, making it the largest beekeeping outfit in Thailand.) Phaothai sells most of his extracted honey to Taiwan. Because the honey has a high moisture content, he dehydrates it (using a process developed by the Chinese) before export. At the extraction site, I am impressed by the amount of product. Everywhere I look, "liquid sunlight" is stored in buckets and barrels. A staff of twelve, mostly young people, harvest about thirty to forty kilos of honey per hive. At this site alone, there are forty hives. Honey means money. After the filming, we return to the factory for snacks, beer and sparkling wine, with Phaothai as our congenial host. Phaothai decides to take us to lunch at a "floating" restaurant. We all pile into several vehicles for the short drive. From the parking lot, we walk across a foot bridge. The restaurant is surrounded by water, giving the illusion that it is floating. The restaurant's heavy-duty furniture is made from cattle yokes and wagon wheels. I expect Clint Eastwood to walk in at any minute.

Some people eat to live, but I'm beginning to think that Thais live to eat. Manas and Phaothai handle all the ordering. Given the length of their discussion with the waiter, I expect multiple courses, and I am not disappointed. Pork curry, fish served in two styles (baked and fried), sticky rice, fried pork rind, green papaya salad, green mango salad, and plates of fresh lettuce and sliced cucumbers. A side bowl of the appropriate sauce accompanies each fish and meat dish. We wash it all down with copious amounts of Singha beer. This is what Mike calls a long lunch, meaning it's late in the afternoon when we finish.

I'm completely sated and satisfied—fat and happy, as the saying goes. Just as I'm thinking how good it will be to get back to the apartment and take it easy, Mike informs me that we have a wedding reception to attend! So, it's back to the lab for us, where we splash some water on our faces, hop on Mike's trusty motorbike, and head to the reception. As it turns out, we don't know the bride or the groom, but needless to say, weddings are a big deal in Thailand. We're here as guests of the Old Goat Band, which has been invited to provide the music for the post-ceremonies banquet.

The Old Goat Band consists mainly of retired gentlemen, with the notable exception of Pornthawee, the Singing Nurse, who accompanied Mike and me to the zoo. According to Mike, Manas is rather famous, at least in the north of the country, as a singer of traditional Thai music, old style. Mike refers to him as the John Denver of Northern Thailand, but his repertoire consists chiefly of Thai folk songs. Pornthawee sings folk songs, too, but she also sings a number of western pop songs.

Over the next several hours, we enjoy the music, some more food and drink, and the general atmosphere of the celebration. Whenever the band takes a short break, Manas comes over to sit and talk with us. We meet the married couple, act like we belong, and have a wonderful time. Wedding crashers, Thai style. As far as I can tell, nobody minds us being here.

It's well after midnight when we return to Mike's apartment, and I'm keenly aware that we must be up early tomorrow. We're going to spend the morning in the lab, searching for *Varroa* mites. Even so, I can't go straight to bed. What a jam-packed, intense, and wonderful day! My mind is racing. I'm keeping up with the fast pace, trying my best to experience everything the Monkey Brothers talk about, take me to, or give me to eat. I want to live this adventure to the fullest. Eventually, though, the adrenaline wears off, and I realize: I am exhausted. Time to sleep.

WEEK FOUR

Our route takes us along the old highway, a narrow and winding two-lane road. For a distance of about four miles, the highway is lined on both sides with very old, mature dipterocarp trees. . . . I stare out the window, transfixed by the loveliness of the aged sentinels. I am fifty-one years of age. My hair is graying. Various aches and pains are daily reminders of athletic injuries suffered decades ago. And still, I am literally a babe in the woods here.

Mike checking a hive for mite infestation, Chiang Mai, Thailand, March 1996.

Sunday, March 10th

Back at the lab, with the Aussie crew on hand, Mike and I are microscopically examining drones we have removed from comb brood cells of the eastern honey bee, the adapted host for these parasites. Some of the drones are larva and some are adults. Before I begin, I silently apologize to the bees. The fact is, I *am* sorry for taking any life, and I don't do it lightly. I understand, though, that this research might help their species to survive. And so, I think it's necessary. We find a total of three *Varroa* mites—Mike, one; Jake, two! Bruce and Phil are ecstatic. They're able to film the entire process of locating, removing, and examining the *Varroa* mites.

I rarely get the chance to participate in scientific research; that's just not the focus of my career. And yet I've thoroughly enjoyed the morning. I've always found microscopic examinations both fascinating and satisfying. It's good to re-acquaint myself with the world of research, if only for a brief time, and I'm thankful that Mike provided me with this opportunity.

After my morning in the lab, I do a mental one-hundred-eighty-degree turn when, at 10:00 am, the Singing Nurse picks me up at the lab. She has something to share with me, she says, smiling broadly. Off we go. I'm delighted when I learn that our destination is Wat Umong, my favorite of all the temples I've visited. When we reach the temple, the Singing Nurse tells me that it is time for some quiet reflection about religion in general and Buddhism in particular. We walk slowly around the grounds, visiting the "talking trees." We read together: "Buddha Dharma is not the religion of everyone who calls himself a Buddhist. For many are found who call themselves Buddhists but do not conduct their lives according to the Dharma as taught by Gutama Buddha." She explains that the Dharma can mean truth, uprightness, correctness, or teaching—specifically, the teaching of the Buddha.

We read further: "Christianity is not the religion of everyone who calls himself a Christian. For many are found who call themselves Christians but do not conduct their lives according to the Dharma as taught by Jesus Christ." Once again, the Singing Nurse repeats: "Dharma can mean truth, uprightness, correctness, or teaching—specifically, the teaching of Christ."

"People of other religions often fall into the same pattern," she says. We read together "But all human beings, regardless of age or sex, desire happiness. They try to avoid hate and suffering. That is why they take refuge in religion." We conclude our reading. "This being so, why in the world do men have prejudices against one another—all because of the difference of names of their religious founders."

We find a bench and sit in quiet contemplation. I had no idea then how many times—but surely it has been hundreds—I would think about what we read and discussed during that temple visit.

After what seems like no more than a few minutes, the Singing Nurse touches my arm and tells me it's time to go. Only then do I realize that we have been sitting in near silence for more than an hour. "Are you hungry?" she asks in her quiet, unassuming voice. "It's time for lunch."

In minutes, we arrive at her apartment, where the Singing Nurse has cooked a homemade meal, a most wonderful soup of rice with a broth thick with both shrimp and crabmeat. It's absolutely delicious. Maybe it's the day's experiences—satisfying both my scientific and religious curiosities—but it is the best meal I've had in Thailand.

The Singing Nurse offers to drive me back to CMU, but I opt to walk. It's good to stretch my legs, and walking gives me time to process my day. Maybe it's the regular rhythm of the walking motion, maybe it's the extra oxygen to the brain—whatever the reason, I think best when I walk. By the time I reach the lab, it's late afternoon. Mike is gone, and he's left a note for me on the door: "Jake, meet me outside at 5:00 pm for dinner." Ah yes, I remember now. The Associate Dean of Science is taking us (Mike, me, and Manas) to a well-known restaurant in the foothills south of Chiang Mai. I have a little downtime, so I head outside for a stroll around campus.

Shortly before 5:00 pm, I return to the lab building and meet up with Mike and Manas. We take Manas's car. The drive takes us along a winding road that looks out onto a beautiful valley. Up on the hillsides, numerous small brush fires are burning. It's the dry season, and such fires are common, Mike tells me. Nobody pays any attention to them, as they burn themselves out on their own, but they are a seasonal contributor to the hazy atmosphere of the Chiang Mai valley. That haze was first commented on by an eighteenth-century French surveyor hired by the King at the time, to map the northern region of Thailand. In the intervening centuries, the addition of exhaust from internal combustion engines has compounded the "smokiness" of the region.

When we arrive at the restaurant, I'm reminded of Ohio's state park lodges. (There's one just fifteen minutes or so from Oxford, in Hueston Woods State Park.) I'm not sure why, but perhaps it's the setting, the structure itself, or the long, lovely drive we made to get there. Or all three.

Turns out the restaurant is owned by a bank and is used as a resort training center. Dinner includes multiple courses—I lose count of the dishes—and lasts several hours. Manas insists on ordering for the table. Fine with me. I want an authentic experience, and Manas does not disappoint! I'm not even sure what I'm eating most of the time, but the overall experience is one of a visually pleasing, taste-bud-erupting, mouth-on-fire feast! I love most of the dishes, but I find a few nearly inedible. If there's one thing I've learned about Thai cooking, it's this: No source of protein goes to waste. If it contains carbon, they will find a way to make a meal of it.

Like most Thais, Manas is fond of spicy cuisine. His pleasure is evident by the streams of sweat running down his face. Dr. Jarupan is a lovely dining companion. Well-educated, well-read, and possessing the indefinable charm of a Thai woman. As it turns out, she was married to an American and for a time lived in Syracuse, New York. Her husband died tragically at a relatively early age, so she returned to Chiang Mai to take up an administrative position at CMU.

We're back at the apartment by 10:30 pm. Mike tells me we have just enough time to get ready for the Chiang Mai fireworks display. It's a big deal, he explains. Tonight's display is part of a nationwide celebration for the Thai Princess Mother Srinagarindra, affectionately known as Somdet Ya, or "the Royal Grandmother." A much-beloved figure, and one of the longest-living royals, she was a strong advocate for education, public health, and conservation. She spearheaded a number of projects to better conditions for the hill tribes of the country's mountainous north, so much so that they consider her their special patron and refer to her as Mae Fah Luang, "Royal Mother from the Sky" or "Heavenly Royal Mother."

Mike continues to fill me in on recent Thai history. The Princess Mother passed away the previous year, on July 18th, 1995, but in keeping with Buddhist custom, and as befitting a royal, the mourning period for her death has been lengthy—in this case, more than eight months. The mourning will come to a fantastic climax this evening, at 11:00 pm, when the Princess Mother's son, King Bhumibol Adulyadej, will light the funeral pyre containing her remains. The pyre is part of an elaborately carved crematorium built to symbolize the mythical mountain home of the Hindu gods. (An interesting sidenote, Mike points out, is that Thai royal funeral ceremonies are a fascinating mix of beliefs—Buddhist, Hindu, and animistic.) The crematorium was erected in a royal field near the Grand Palace in the heart of Bangkok's historic district. Thousands of people have crowded Bangkok's streets and the area around the palace to watch the festivities, which are being televised to watchers throughout Thailand. Indeed, it seems the entire country is pausing tonight to pay homage to the Princess Mother. At wats nationwide, symbolic funeral pyres also will be lit at 11:00 pm, accompanied by pyrotechnics displays. Mike's eighth-floor apartment, with its panoramic view to the south, affords us a front-row seat to Chiang Mai's celebration. As the clock ticks the eleventh hour, colorful fireworks begin to light up the southern sky over Wat Suan Dok, one of the more famous temples in Chiang Mai. Mike and I toast the Princess Mother with cold beers and wish her well on her journey.

Monday, March 11th

Not much is planned for today. Mike will be busy with administrative duties all day; I won't see him until 5:00 pm. Bruce and Phil are off filming some additional bee footage, which includes mature colonies of dwarf honey bees that Mike has transplanted on the shady side of his lab and a giant honey bee colony that is nesting on the overhang of the fourth floor of the main building of the College of Agriculture. With their long lenses, the Aussies have told us there will be no problem getting some close-ups. I'm going to spend time reading this morning, then have lunch with Hans Bänziger. Swiss by nationality, Hans has worked in Thailand for more than thirty years. Mike tells me that Hans is an entomologist who is currently working on native slipper orchid pollination, which he studies by ascending the tall dipterocarp trees in the forest where the orchids are found. Orchids are among a group of plants known as epiphytes, plants that grow on top of, or attach themselves to, other plants, often trees. They derive their nutrients and water from the air, water, dust, and debris around them. Unlike parasites, they don't harm the host on which they grow. Because epiphytes don't grow in soil (though they may get their start in leaf debris or moss caught in between the branches of a tree), they are sometimes called "air plants." I want to talk with Hans about his work and impressions of environmental issues in Thailand. For now, I'm spending the morning listening to Jim Croce (apparently popular in Thailand) and Paul Simon sing love songs on the radio.

I've been taking a lot of deep breaths, trying to decompress a little after the last three days. It's nice to be on my own. My walk to the campus is pleasant enough. I've learned a route with a minimum of traffic. My comfort level, my confidence level, and my sense of purpose are all the highest they've been since I arrived here weeks ago.

Outside the library, I pick up copies of the *Bangkok Post*. In our textbook, *The Biosphere: Protecting Our Global Environment*, my co-author Cecilia Berg and I developed a method for classifying environmental issues into one of three categories: population, pollution, or resource abuse. (Often, an issue will fit into two or even all three categories.) The classification helps students make sense of the endless stream of environmental issues, and more importantly, it allows us to show how the categories are interrelated, which explains why environmental issues are so complex and difficult to solve or prevent.

I'm going to see how our classification holds up by trying to find examples in Thai newspapers. For population issues, I find articles on AIDS, condom use, and the need for more services and resources for a fast-growing economy fueled by an increase in young adults. For pollution issues, I find an article about carp dying in the ponds on Parliament grounds; the fish kill was traced to increased bacteria counts and high chlorine levels in the water. A second article discusses the obstacles to reducing air pollution, citing legal loopholes and vagueness in the clean air laws, along with lax enforcement and buck-passing. For resource abuse, I find an article on land use. Farmers are losing their rights to farm common land (public land) that they had been using and stewarding for decades, in favor of major projects like roads, dams, and reservoirs. The articles, of course, are weighty, but I feel good knowing that even in Thailand, our classification system works. I've taken notes on everything I've read, so I'll be able to use my research here to further inform my teaching.

Time passes quickly. While I'm engrossed in my newspapers, the noon hour sneaks up on me. I hurry across campus to find Hans waiting for me at the lab. Hans frequently visits the bee lab, often consulting with Mike on insect identification and advising him on the best ways to navigate the waters of higher education in Thailand.

Hans is single, no family except for a sister; thus, he has no responsibilities beyond himself and his work. He enjoys the freedom to do his work in the forest on his own schedule. Hans is also a bit of an activist. He recently spoke out against a proposed cable car project and hotel that would intrude on the forest that blankets much of the zoo grounds. According to Hans, there is an activist group waiting to "wake up" when the Thai environment needs protection.

I'm impressed and intrigued by Hans. Here's a scientist/naturalist working, in his own gentle way, to protect the forest he has come to know and love. But it's his passion for rare plants, particularly orchids, and the time he takes in the mountainous forest to find, describe and catalogue them, that most fascinates me. Hans spends days upon days tramping through the forest, on his own, sometimes sleeping there overnight in all kinds of weather, searching for orchids—orchids in all their splendor, in the infinite variety much prized by collectors. He is trying to understand the biology and ecology of as many species as he can find before they disappear from their natural habitat. As a scientist, he's conflicted. Science progresses, in large part, because scientists share what they learn with other scientists through peer-reviewed papers and presentations. But Hans is reluctant to reveal what he learns for fear that his information might enable collectors to locate and remove the orchids from the wild. And so, he hesitates to publish his work or even to keep detailed notes.

Hans feels, as I do, that most people believe nature is good only when humans put it to some use. For most people, experiencing nature on its own isn't enough; there must be some economics involved, something to *do* with it. Some money to be made somewhere, somehow.

Hans tells me a story to emphasize his point. He has rented his house for fifteen years. He wanted both the house and the yard to have a "natural" look, but one of his British visitors thought the place needed tidying up. He mentioned that to the owner, who then decided to hire a gardener to "fix up" the grounds in an effort to make it more appealing—more marketable—to potential renters. The owner's idea of improving the grounds meant replacing the native plants with exotic ones and ensuring that everything was neat and manicured—hardly conducive to a natural system, but an "aesthetic" that might bring in more rentals.

Since Hans spends so much time in the forest, I bring up my observation about all of the toilet paper I observed on my hike. His shoulders slump, his facial expression darkens, and his gaze drops to his hands. "A lot of people don't care about the toilet paper, the human waste, the other litter on the forest paths. . . . " His voice trails off, and we're both quiet for a moment. Without a word, we start for the door.

Hans has a favorite noodle restaurant near the campus, and we are both happy for the walk. The restaurant is small but clean and inviting. I order a fried noodle dish, and it's wonderful. My Thai friends have never brought me here. I suspect they believe noodles are "too common," much as rice is considered to be in the finer restaurants in China. We finish, walk about a block, and Hans treats me to ice cream—another on my growing list of reasons to appreciate this intriguing individual. He is certainly more interesting than I was led to believe, and he's given me much to think about. I look forward to telling Mike about my day and my observations. For now, I'm ready to return to the apartment, glad for a couple of hours alone to process my thoughts.

Twenty-five years later, as Mike and I collaborate on this book, Mike informs me that much has changed for Hans, even as much remains the same. Hans is married now—to the former head secretary of the entomology department. They have built a lovely home at the base of Doi Suthep, in an area of remaining forest. As passionate as ever about orchids in particular and wild things in general, Hans continues his various research projects and has been formally awarded a courtesy faculty position in the entomology department at CMU.

Tuesday, March 12th

This morning, Mike and I visit an old orchard outside the town of Mae Rim, ten miles north of Chiang Mai. The owner has transplanted dwarf honey bee colonies from outlying areas and then tied them onto his longan, litchi, and mango trees. He loves the bees in and of themselves, but he is also savvy enough to understand that the hives greatly enhance pollination and fruit production. Talk about a win-win situation! We have to cross a rickety bamboo bridge to get to the orchard. The orchard workers are afraid I won't make it across the bridge. I look old to them, probably because of my white beard. They've taken to calling me grandpa!

As we walk toward the orchard, Mike tells me a little about dwarf honey bees. Two species of dwarf honey bees inhabit Southeast Asia and both are subject to significant predation by humans. The bee hunters take everything except the adult bees. You can often find the colonies with honey and brood for sale in local village markets. He explains that while dwarf honey bees are usually gentle, intrusions too close to their colonies can put them into a defensive posture, and they have a nasty sting. So, I hang back while Mike gets a close look. In the process, he is stung several times. As Mike hops around in discomfort, I notice the orchard workers getting a good laugh at his expense.

As we leave the orchard, we walk by a field planted with hot Thai peppers. According to the orchard workers, the peppers are "the hottest of the hot." I get enough seeds to share with my friend Clark, a hot pepper aficionado. Clark specializes in Oh God sauces. When you first taste them, your initial reaction is an astounded "Oh God!" I enjoy growing peppers of all kinds; cultivating these will be fun.

After our visit, we head back to the apartment to change. Along with Prachaval, we are having dinner at a local restaurant with Manas and his family. Manas's wife is the dean of the College of Pharmacy at CMU. I sit next to the children, Manas's thirteen-year-old son, Jim, and his fifteen-year-old daughter, Yui. Mike and Manas both explain to me that Jim is very shy and normally refuses to talk to anyone other than his immediate family. I'm pleased and a little humbled when he and I connect straight away. We carry on a conversation that lasts through dinner. I invite him to visit Oxford for the three months of summer or even for the school year. Since he loves soccer, naturally, the sport features prominently in our conversation. He invites me to watch him play; unfortunately, I will be returning home before his next game. I invite Manas to visit Oxford also. It would give me a chance to repay his many kindnesses to me. He loves to fish, and all of the fishing we've done here in Thailand has helped to forge a bond between us.

It is a wonderful family outing, one that makes me realize how much I miss my own family back home. Years later, I learn that Manas's son earned a law degree at CMU and his daughter earned a medical degree. Both are now married and enjoying successful, productive lives.

Mike, Prachaval, Manas, and I remain at the restaurant for after-dinner drinks while Manas's wife takes the children home. We are joined for drinks by Phaothai, who, after a while, suggests we go to the massage house to end the day. This will be my third visit. I smile inwardly. I knew it was coming—a third "test," as it were.

We return to the second massage house we visited weeks ago. Nothing is said, but I can tell my friends are having difficulty understanding my celibacy. They do not address it directly, and I don't get the sense they are being critical. More puzzled than anything. In their minds, they are simply giving me an opportunity to experience the very thing that many men come to Thailand for. But I'm not interested. Whether they respect me for not taking part, or are simply baffled, I'm not sure, but they never ask why. So, after a few beers and a lot of cashew nuts, one of the feathered singers visits our table. (Tonight, we were not in the main room with the "women behind the glass.") They explain to her in Thai that I am "too shy and polite" for a "massage." Actually, my reasons are much more complex, but I don't feel the need to explain. They're my friends; they don't judge me for my choices, just as I don't judge them for theirs. But as I have said before, my decision is based on respect—for my wife, for women in general. I do not make promises lightly.

While sex is not in the cards tonight, I am interested in a traditional Thai massage, reputed to be among the most effective of all massage therapies. I've been wanting one for weeks, ever since the day Manas took me to lunch and the subject first came up. No problem, Manas says. A few words to the feathered singer, and minutes later, another woman appears. Mike agrees to join me, and we follow her down a hall and up a flight of stairs. We enter a small room that has two bamboo mats on the floor, one for him, one for me. She gives each of us a cold beer. We remove our shoes, but nothing else, lie down and make ourselves comfortable. Two massage girls—women deemed "too old" to be prostitutes—enter the room. Amazing. They can't be older than their late twenties or early thirties. The women proceed to give us a bone-cracking massage. We are prodded, twisted, and bent into positions I would never have dreamt possible! It isn't painful, exactly, but it hovers just on the brink of pain. It is the deepest massage I have *ever* had. As I said, Thais are known for their deep massages.

As we are getting the massage, Mike and I notice that the women are watching television the whole time. Mike understands enough Thai to realize they are watching a soap opera. When he tells me this, we both break out in uncontrollable laughter. The girls are so disinterested in us that they could immerse themselves in television drama while administering this tough, deep massage.

After they finish, Mike and I sit up and lean back against a wall. Suddenly, the girls address Mike. They ask him if they can feel my beard. I agree, and they giggle with delight. I'm reminded, once again, of how foreign I look to people here. I'm not accustomed to standing out, to being noticed for my appearance. Even though I've traveled abroad, I suppose it's always been to places where I blend in more easily. For maybe the first time in my life, I'm in the minority here. It's a strange experience, but one I'm grateful for.

When we're ready, we stand, go downstairs to meet our friends, pay our tab, and leave. As we go, I learn that, tomorrow, at his wife's suggestion, Manas is taking me to "the elephant training center." Whatever that is.

Wednesday, March 13th

The Elephant Training and Work Site Center is a tourist attraction, and normally, I avoid tourist attractions. I remind myself, however, that I'm here to experience Thailand to the fullest, and if Manas's wife thinks that I should see the center, then I shall go and see the center.

I feel fortunate to have Manas as my guide. On the way, we talk about fishing and sports. He loves both. Says if he had known earlier that I like sports so much, he would have invited me to a kickboxing competition he went to earlier in the week. Mike doesn't care much for competitive sports, and Manas assumed I would feel the same way. He seems surprised at the many differences between Mike and me, given how close we are. Maybe it's a Monkey Brothers trait—the appreciation for people and things different from one's self. I'd like to think so.

It turns out that Manas was a semi-pro kickboxer during his undergraduate days. The money he earned helped pay for the costs of his degree. I'm not surprised. Manas's build reminds me of a beer keg. Like most Thais, he's not very tall, but he's strong and stout. Barrel-chested. He's the kind of person I would want on my side in the event of a physical altercation.

Later, when I tell Mike about my day, he explains that Manas comes from a very humble background. His father was a samlor driver, a samlor being the traditional three-wheeled bicycle taxi. Unfortunately, the samlor is slowly disappearing in favor of motorized taxis. That the son of a samlor driver should become a respected university professor is unusual, to put it mildly. In Thailand, higher education is in a *de facto* manner limited to children of the upper middle class and above. It was only because of Manas's impressive intellect that he was allowed to attend a decent high school, acquire the necessary English skills to score high on the national university entrance examination, and ultimately, to enroll at CMU. After graduation, he was awarded a scholarship from the Ford Foundation, which enabled him to earn his PhD at Utah State University. Manas's inspiring story is one of perseverance and drive, and it underscores the importance of education in changing the trajectory of peoples' lives. Manas's wife is a member of a high-ranking family from Lamphun, a province adjacent to Chiang Mai. Prior to the union of present-day Thailand late in the eighteenth century, Lamphun was a separate principality. Her family's connections go as high as the Royal family. Mike tells me that, on their wedding day, Manas and his wife were invited to dine with the King and Queen at the royal Winter Palace, which sits at the very top of Doi Suthep.

Back to my morning. A steady stream of elephants and tourists mingle freely at the center. The Elephant Training and Work Site Center is definitely the most touristy place I've been thus far, but Manas's wife has instructed him to take me away from the tourists for a more in-depth experience. First, though, we take a seat in the stands to watch the elephants perform. It's an interesting show, with lots of tricks and balancing and working with logs (as they would in the forest.) The elephants also play "soccer," kicking a giant flexible ball around the arena. To the audience's delight, one elephant kicks the ball out of the arena. A German man agrees to lay down on the arena floor while an elephant places its foot on his chest. Whew! We leave the arena and walk the grounds, the elephants and visitors again mixing freely throughout the center. Scores of tourists and dozens of adult elephants, including some with people aboard and some with their babies walking alongside, ebb and flow around us. I've never seen anything like it. I can't even imagine anything like this being allowed in the US. The risk of an accident—and the inevitable lawsuit—is far too high. At one point, we quickly move to the side, so that an elephant with people going for a ride can pass us on the confluence of two trails.

Manas leads me away from the crowd to a more secluded part of the compound. There, we walk past individual elephants confined to pens. Thankfully, the pens are constructed under large trees, so the elephants are in the shade all day. These are the stressed, sick, or injured elephants that have been removed from their work sites in the forest and brought here for treatment, recuperation, and rest. Each elephant has an individual prescription. In a quiet voice, Manas reads four treatments to me. Elephant #1, medicine, rest, and massage; Elephant #2, salve for the feet, rest, and massage; Elephant #3, rest and massage; Elephant #4, salve for the skin and massage.

Manas asks me if I want to ride an elephant. I don't. But I do want a closer look. I ask Manas if it's alright to touch one of the elephants, and he says yes. I choose number #4, the elephant being treated with a salve for the skin and massage. I place my hand on his side and look into his magnificent eye. In the past several decades, animal behaviorists have learned a great deal about elephants, and their findings are fascinating.

Elephants are extremely intelligent animals; they can learn new facts and behaviors, mimic sounds, self-medicate, play, use tools and perform artistic endeavors, such as painting pictures. They also are capable of a range of emotions, including joy, playfulness, and grief. They seem to have a sense of humor; they display compassion; they mourn; and they exhibit self-awareness. The elephant's brain is the largest of any animal—it's more than twice the size of the brain of the blue whale (the world's largest animal), even though the latter has a body size twenty times as large as the elephant. The neocortex of the elephant brain—the area of the mammalian brain responsible for working memory, planning, and problem solving—is highly convoluted, just as it is in the brains of humans, apes, and some dolphins. A highly convoluted neocortex is considered a sign of complex intelligence. One of the few species not born with survival instincts (humans are another), elephants must learn them during their infancy and adolescence. Fortunately, they have a long lifespan, similar to that of humans, affording them ample time, roughly ten years, to acquire the "life learning" needed to be considered adults.

Standing so closely to this magnificent creature, I feel a sense of awe and wonder. His gaze is calming, and there is a remarkable depth in his eyes that literally takes my breath away. Quietly, I wish him a thorough recovery and a safe journey through life.

I understand now why Manas's wife insisted I visit the center.

We return to have lunch at the faculty club of Chiang Mai University. I'm not sure why we haven't eaten here before. The food is good, it's cheap, and it's close to the lab. Manas ordered two special dishes for me. One is fresh *laab* produced from CMU beef cattle in the Department of Animal Science, and it's best described as heavily spiced chopped beef. Some people prefer it uncooked, but not today.

Manas seems to have taken an interest in me. I like him, perhaps most of all the people I've met in Thailand. He can be both crude and gentle. I'll never forget meeting his mother and the kind, compassionate, and respectful way he treated her.

Back at the lab, I run into Phil, the Aussie team leader. He offers to take me to tea before my flight leaves on Friday and to pay for my overnight stay in Bangkok. As much as I'd like to accept the tea invitation, my time is short. And as far as the hotel payment goes, I know Phil is trying to compensate me for my help with the mite work. He doesn't realize that the opportunity to meet him and his crew, to do laboratory work again and to help with his important project, is payment enough. Maybe his film will do the trick to educate Australian beekeepers and motivate politicians so that they prevent *Varroa* and *Tropilaelaps* infestations in Australia's hives. If that's so, Mike will have played a major part in the prevention and I will have had a tiny part. Good enough for me.

Tonight, Mike and I eat dinner at Manas's home. His wife believes I am good with their children. It's a lovely evening. They have prepared a variety of dishes from fish, meat, and vegetables purchased at the morning food market.

I don't know if I'll ever meet the members of this family again. I do know I will carry them in my heart, always.

Thursday, March 14th

Today, Mike tells me, I will be treated to a going-away celebration. It's late afternoon when we set off for the nearby town of Lamphun, located in Lamphun province. Our route takes us along the old highway, a narrow and winding two-lane road. For a distance of about four miles, the highway is lined on both sides with very old, mature dipterocarp trees. A family of hardwood, tropical trees comprising some nearly seven hundred species, dipterocarps are climax species in the forests of Southeast Asia. For a biologist, the experience is thrilling. I stare out the window, transfixed by the loveliness of the aged sentinels. I am fifty-one years of age. My hair is graying. Various aches and pains are daily reminders of athletic injuries suffered decades ago. And still, I am literally a babe in the woods here.

Like ecosystems everywhere—grasslands or wetlands for example—forests change over time. Through a process that biologists call ecological succession, one plant community gives way to another, until, eventually, the result is a mix of species best suited to the physical conditions (temperature, precipitation, soil type, etc.) of the area. These best-suited species are known as climax species, and as long as a site remains undisturbed, the composition of those species remains essentially unchanged. In Thailand, as elsewhere throughout this region, those species are mostly dipterocarps. In Southwest Ohio, the climax species in most forests are beech and maple, though oaks and hickories may dominate in the drier soils of slopes and ravines.

Mike tells me that dipterocarps are also a favorite tree substrate for giant honey bees to nest on. About every tenth tree has bamboo pegs driven into the trunk; the pegs form a ladder that allows bee hunters to reach the nests during the harvest season. According to traditional culture, bee hunters have the rights to individual trees. A few months from now, when the harvest is ready, this road will be, well, busy as a bee, but today, it's quiet. We see no one—no motorized vehicles, no bicycles, no walkers—as we travel through the living tunnel created by these towering giants.

My mind is still back amongst the trees when we arrive at the restaurant. We're joined by the members of the Old Goat Band, including Manas and Odie. It's a wonderful evening. The band sings dozens of songs for me; they sing before we eat, during the long meal, and again after we eat. The array of dishes is almost overwhelming. I'd have thought that after a month in Thailand, eating out several times a day, there would be few dishes or courses left to experience, and yet the night is full of culinary surprises. My most adventurous attempt to eat new things occurred when the waiter brought fried bamboo worms. They look something like mealworms, which I often use in my teaching. The server brought us a communal bowl; in one fluid motion, we put our fingers in the bowl, grabbed a healthy number, tossed our heads back, and dropped them into our mouths. At least they weren't wiggling! As I bit into the bunch, my mouth filled with what seemed like warm oil. The bamboo worms are rich in fats, and they have the consistency of melted butter—but without the good butter taste. Even so, everyone seemed to enjoy the sensation, as did I.

After we finish eating, and after the last song is sung, I am given a special going-away gift: A small image (3/4 inch x 1 1/4 inch x 1/4 inch) of the Pa Le Li Buddha. It depicts an elephant offering the Buddha water, while a monkey offers the Buddha a honeycomb. Manas explains that it refers to the moment when the Buddha emerged from his long fast, having achieved the enlightenment he sought. My friends and fellow Monkey Brothers purchased the image from a temple in the south of Thailand that is devoted to this loving act by the elephant and the monkey. They tell me that the image possesses extreme good karma and should always be kept close. I treasure this gift, given as it is with great love and affection. I intend to always keep it close and do my best to add to its karma.

Friday, March 15th

I awaken early, eager to savor every minute of my last day in Chiang Mai. Over a simple breakfast of fresh fruit and coffee, Mike and I check my travel itinerary. My flight from Chiang Mai to Bangkok leaves a little after 10:00 pm, with an ETA in the nation's capital 11:00 pm. I'll spend the night at the Bangkok airport, and early tomorrow, I'll begin the long journey home. Flights from Bangkok to Tokyo; Tokyo to Detroit, Michigan; and Detroit to Dayton, Ohio. Pat will pick me up at the Dayton airport on Sunday morning for the last leg of my journey, an hour-long drive home to Oxford.

We spend most of the day in and around the apartment, talking, laughing, and making plans for our next adventure together—or perhaps for a second Monkey Brothers adventure. Who knows? I do a couple loads of wash, happy to pack clean clothing in my bags. We grab lunch from a street vendor, and later, have a leisurely dinner at the nearby Solao restaurant. It's well after 7:00 pm before we walk back to Mike's apartment and I gather my things.

To the airport and away. Most of the Monkey Brothers have come to see me off and to wish me a safe trip home. We hug and kiss and hug some more. Mike is the last to embrace me.

"Jake, you're a good shit."

"You're a good shit, too, Mike."

EPILOGUE

As I write these words, nearly twenty-five years after the events recounted in *The Monkey Brothers Adventures in Thailand*, I'm astonished at how vivid the memories still are. Sometimes, it seems as if my journey was just last year. The sights, the sounds, the smells, the people, the animals . . . Thailand imprinted itself on my brain. And in my heart.

The world is a very different place than it was in 1996, and yet, much remains the same. Mike is still doing basic and applied research, now on multiple species of bees, and he is still teaching at Oregon State University. He returns to Thailand late each December, remaining there until mid-March, and then returns to the US to teach an honors course in the spring quarter. He remains an incredibly productive researcher. In many ways, publications are the currency of academics, the standard by which we assess one's scholarship and contributions to science. By that standard, Mike is a wealthy man. He has authored or co-authored over one hundred peer-reviewed publications. He's also mentored nearly twenty graduate entomology students and his honors class, "Far Side Entomology," was named "Best College Course in the Country" by none other than Playboy Magazine! Mike is first and foremost a dedicated scientist. Scientific research is the backbone and driver of his long and distinguished career—a career that has contributed significantly to our understanding of honey bees and other bee species.

Like many others, I've been thinking about science and scientists a *lot* lately. With the COVID-19 pandemic and the climate crisis dominating the news and our lives, it's hard *not* to think about science. There is no doubt: Scientific discovery can vastly improve the human condition in myriad ways—but *only* if we *listen* to scientists and heed their warnings. If not, we might as well go back to incantations, spells, and "cures" like blood-letting. Shot of bleach, anyone? To put it another way, scientists can arm us with information and knowledge, but they can't force us to accept it or to use it. That's up to us. And hopefully, that's where education comes in. In our schools, in our homes, in our offices, in our social circles. We must educate ourselves on the pressing issues of our day—which cannot be done by looking to the questionable sources found on social media. Rather, we must find reputable, thoughtful news sources and learn as much as we can. If a majority of people do that, we'll be much better off in the ways that really count—healthier, safer, more secure.

As for me, I retired in 2015 after fifty years of teaching at all levels of education from fifth-grade through post-graduate work. (As the Director of Miami University's Museum of Natural History, I also taught special classes and programs for preschoolers, and I spent more than twenty years working with practicing elementary and high school teachers, so my students have ranged from three to sixty-plus years of age.) Presently, I am the Executive Director of the Salt Creek Nature Sanctuary. Forty-five minutes southwest of Oxford, Ohio, in southeastern Indiana's Franklin County, the sanctuary was formerly a hill farm. The land has not been cultivated since my wife, Patricia, and I purchased it in 1983. In the ensuing decades, the old farm has reverted to a wild, natural state, and the Sanctuary is now a 280-acre tapestry of mature woodlands and healthy fields. A pond, small creeks, and numerous vernal pools grace its gently rolling hills, sheltered valleys, and rugged ravines. The sanctuary is a true labor of love, something Pat and I share with each other, our dog (Tess), our families and our friends, but it is something we *give* to the future. In 2007, we signed over the deed to the Salt Creek Nature Sanctuary to The Oxford Society (TOS), a non-profit we established, to manage it in perpetuity. In my spare time, I am the managing partner of Two Herons Consulting and Berg Kaufman Publishing, both of which I established with my long-time colleague and co-author, Cecilia Berg.

Over the years, the friendship Mike and I share has grown stronger, cemented by our incredible adventure in Thailand in 1996. What makes our friendship so strong? From the beginning, we have accepted one another for who we are, despite the differences in our backgrounds. Even though our professional paths diverged—Mike focused on research, agricultural extension service, and teaching, and I focused on nature study and environmental issues, teaching, and service to practicing teachers—our friendship remains solid. Just as both paths had their "trailheads," so to speak, in our education at Edinboro, our friendship is rooted in the bonds we formed as first-year students nearly sixty years ago. It's endured because we've never been critical or judgmental of one another, and we've respected each other's path in life. Sometimes, years pass before we see one another. But when we do get together, we take up where we left off, as if we'd seen each other the week before. Our friendship is the proverbial pair of old, comfortable shoes—the fit is perfect, they don't hurt your feet, and you never tire of the style.

About the Authors

A native of Pittsburgh, Pennsylvania, Donald Kaufman retired from teaching in 2016 after having spent fifty years as an educator at all levels—from preK and grade school through college and graduate school. Presently, Don is the Executive Director of The Oxford Society, a nonprofit organization he and his wife, Patricia, established in 2003. The Kaufmans and their dog, Tess, divide their time between their home in Oxford, Ohio, and the Salt Creek Nature Sanctuary in Franklin County, Indiana. The sanctuary is owned and operated by The Oxford Society and spans more than 280 acres of rolling, wooded countryside interspersed with fields and meadows.

A native of Edinboro, Pennsylvania, Michael Burgett is a professor emeritus at Oregon State University. Each spring semester, Mike teaches an honors course at OSU; he spends several months each year at Chiang Mai University in Chiang Mai, Thailand, where he conducts basic and applied research on multiple species of bees. He is also an avid outdoorsman and enjoys hiking and fishing throughout the Pacific Northwest. Mike and his wife, Janice, reside in Corvallis, Oregon.

Made in USA - Crawfordsville, IN
56982_9781732262218
10.08.2021 1657